T0354934

CRYSTAL INSPIRATIONS

POEMS

BY

JoANNE TUTTLE

iUniverse, Inc.
Bloomington

CRYSTAL INSPIRATIONS
Poems by JoAnne Tuttle

Copyright © 2010, 2012 by JoAnne Tuttle

All rights reserved. No part of this book may be used or reproduced by any means, graphic, electronic, or mechanical, including photocopying, recording, taping or by any information storage retrieval system without the written permission of the publisher except in the case of brief quotations embodied in critical articles and reviews.

iUniverse books may be ordered through booksellers or by contacting:

iUniverse
1663 Liberty Drive
Bloomington, IN 47403
www.iuniverse.com
1-800-Authors (1-800-288-4677)

Because of the dynamic nature of the Internet, any web addresses or links contained in this book may have changed since publication and may no longer be valid. The views expressed in this work are solely those of the author and do not necessarily reflect the views of the publisher, and the publisher hereby disclaims any responsibility for them.

Any people depicted in stock imagery provided by Thinkstock are models, and such images are being used for illustrative purposes only.

Certain stock imagery © Thinkstock.

ISBN: 978-1-4502-7261-2 (sc)
ISBN: 978-1-4502-7262-9 (e)

Printed in the United States of America

iUniverse rev. date: 06/15/2012

CONTENTS

CONTENTS

PREFACE

I have believed since high school days when I studied literature, that one of the reasons poetry was so difficult to understand was because there was no background information that went with each poem to tell me "why" the author wrote his poem. With this thought in mind, I introduce my wife's poems.

JoAnne raised three boys, a brunette, a blond and a redhead. She married me in 1971. She worked for the University of Texas Health Science Center in Dallas (UTHSCD) for twenty years until she retired in 1994.

She writes about me and the people she worked with, including doctors, residents, medical record clerks, secretaries, laboratory technicians and other friends. In addition, she writes about her family, her father and mother, siblings and their offspring, her boys and their offspring, her grandmother, herself, holidays, vacations, nature and --- life.
Continued

Some of her poems express deep religious convictions and experiences. Some poems are happy; several are sad; many are funny; and a number of have a deeper moral significance. Most of her poems tell you a great deal about her. All are meant to be enjoyed.

Footnoted to some of her poems, you will be filled in with a little background that inspired its writing; such as the girl who "dropped her drawers (panties) in the middle of the street." Or the time hot coffee was spilled on JoAnne's lap, right close to the "promise-land." Or else, she might tell you to whom that poem was dedicated. I trust this insight will help you enjoy her poems more.

Maybe her poems will make you laugh a little, or feel a little chill bump. It is my hope that you will enjoy sharing her thoughts, experiences and life.

Emery Tuttle
41 years together thus far

TWO LOVE POEMS TO MY WIFE

JoANNE

When the fall of our lives
Turns into winter
I'll be there with
Great anticipation

For the loveliness of you
Now grows day by day, and
With each New Year there's more
Heart and soul participation
Emery Tuttle
02.14.79

"JoANNIE, JoANNIE"

When everything is looking blue
I stop the hurt by thinking you
Will come to me with open arms
And show me of your many charms

Your eyes betray a devilish scheme
And beckon come into your dream
To penetrate that carnal scheme
We can feast on love's sweet dream

"JoAnnie, JoAnnie"
My love is at its best
In "JoAnnie, JoAnnie"
I find my happiness
Emery Tuttle
02.19.79

DEDICATIONS

Initially, let me say there are many things that inspire a poet to write; however, I must dedicate my poetic efforts first to my husband, Emery Tuttle, who is my soul mate. He brought many, many new and wonderful experiences into my life; and without his influence, I would have lived a rather colorless life. Thank you for bringing color, fun, adventures and love into my life, Emery. I had written poetry since childhood, but it was only after we were married that I started to collect and keep my poems.

Second, but not least by any means, I dedicate this book of poetry to my lovely Christian friend and mentor, Crystal Elliott. She inspired and affirmed me to write and influenced me to do my best. Without disparage, condemnation or exaggeration of its value, she always inspired and confirmed my work. She bragged on me and blessed me. Without her "atta-girl," love and encouragement, I, possibly, would not have attempted to publish my poems.
Continued

Thank you for your love, encouragement and Christian influence upon my life, Crystal.

Finally, I must dedicate these poems to all who read them with my sincere hope that you will enjoy sharing in my life and thoughts.

However, in addition, I want to thank the staff at iUniverse for helping this computer-challenged poet to publish.

JoAnne Thompson Holcomb Tuttle

CRYSTAL ELLIOTT

PROVERBS 31:10; 30

"...An excellent wife, who can find?
For her worth is far above jewels...
Charm is deceitful and beauty is vain,
But, a woman who fears the Lord,
She shall be praised..."

A VIRTUOUS WOMAN

Gracious is the word
That *describes* you to a tee
Kindness is the way you act
With everyone you see

If anyone attempts to look
A flaw would not be found
Day and night you're the same
With no one else around

You represent the woman
That every girl should be
You are a virtuous woman
And a gracious friend to me

JoAnne Tuttle 2009

Dedicated to Crystal Elliot with my love, admiration, respect, blessings and my deepest gratitude for your love and inspiration. I miss the fact that we don't live closer to each other.

CRYSTAL INSPIRATIONS

"All About Me"

TUTTLE...
A Name is a Name

Perhaps you've never realized
   I guess I've never said
But I'm just a full-fledge "*Tuttle*"
   From my toes up to my head

Of all the names I could have had
   Of all the names there are
"*Tuttle*" is the name **you** gave me
   And I like it best by far!

Some have called us "*Turtle*"
   And "*Tootle*," "*Tittle*," "*Tuddle*"
But we both know the real truth
   Our name is just plain "*Tuttle*"

Although we get some teasing
...They pun upon our name
No matter what they call us
   I like it all the same

If I had the choice to change it
   To any name I'd choose
There's no other name I like
   There's no other name I'd use

If ever you should leave me
   I would make just one request
I must keep my name "*Tuttle*"
   It's the name I like the best
07.09.73

Dedicated to Emery Tuttle. When we married (12.04.71) I took his name; then when we remarried (07.09.73), JoAnne Tuttle took Emery's name again. I am now JoAnne Tuttle-Tuttle. I like my name. Thank you, Emery.

JoANNE...
Strictly Personal

A most personal thing of mine
   Is of course
   My name -- my sign

Another personal thing in line
   Is my body
   That's strictly mine

But a personal thing I can choose
   Is the time
   I choose to use
02.02.81

A CINDERELLA WISH

A Cinderella-life was my dream
To go to balls and everything
The only things I would not adore
Are all the times she cleaned the floor

It would be nice to have a knight
Who'd chase after me with all his might
Wearing glass slippers would be real neat
However glass slippers might pinch my feet

My own fairy-godmother to grant my whim
Of course I'd like a couple of them
But a stepmom like hers would be no fun
I'm really glad I don't have one

Now the more I think about these dreams
A true nightmare is what it seems
If I could choose whom I'm to be
I must confess, I'd be just *me*
08.01.71

A SIMPLE COMPLEXITY
...That's Me

I've yet to find the real self -- me
   I should be one – it seems I'm three
Because sometimes I see inside
   A little girl who's big, wide-eyed

Then as I look again I see
   She's all grown up -- a woman she
Then quickly now that view is gone
   She changed again; she's not alone

A tow-head boy, a red-head, too
   A head of brown -- three boys I view
Things changed again; these boys are men
   Their own families they will begin

Out of the blue, more bundles of joy
   Five little girls and one little boy
As these six grow, I view my role
   I'm getting gray -- I'm getting old

My life no doubt had changed again
   My little boys were all grown men
Their little families were growing, too
   Then without warning, suddenly I knew

That life-changes will go on and on for me
   At first step one, then two, then three...
Once a simple life I had -- just me
   But now I simply have -- complexity
06.01.71

Notation: My complexity will be revised again and again...as my life continually changes as more complexity is added; however, that complexity also brings me great joy.

4

GREAT-GREAT
GRANDMOTHER – ME
(In her newspaper dress)
JoANNE TUTTLE
2010

GRANDMOTHER? -- Me?

It's hard to be called "grandmother"
When the first grandchild comes along
Because you surely feel so "young"
In *that category* you don't belong

When for the second time around
There's another sweet grandchild
You start getting used to being called
"Grandmother" after a while

It becomes mind-numbing when
The birth of grandchildren first begin
You hear yourself called "grandmother"
Over and over and over and over again

For me the number now has reached
Nine grandkids and still going strong
With number ten on the way
Unless perhaps they're wrong

When there's a choice to make
Between more than two or three
Ordinarily only one grandkid
Your favorite would get to be
Continued

6

I am in a quandary now and
Here's the trouble spot
If only one can be the best
How can I fit nine into that slot?

How then will I decide
Which grandkid is the best?
Because I can't pick just *one*
And leave out all the rest!

Therefore I want each to know
In my eyes they'll always be
The best and number one to me
Because I love each one -- individually
08.01.78

Dedicated to all our grandchildren, (plus a few step-grandchildren we love, too). To date, 1978, we have John, Amy, Joseph, Alicia (01.23.73--07.13.00), Sandra, Tiffany, Casey, Cory, Bradley and now Monique (she is number ten)...after her we now have Cody, Jessica, Marc, Michelle, Gabrielle, Danielle, Jenifer, and Sean. That totals eighteen. Yep, grandmother...that's me! Note: as of printing, (in 2012) three great-great grandchildren have been added ..... (more to come?? You better believe!).

JEREMIAH 1:5

*"Before I formed you in the womb
I knew you; Before you were born
I Sanctified you..."*

LIFE KEEPS ON COMING

It seems it was only a while ago
   I was just a bright-eyed little girl
Then the years went by so fast
   My head went into a spinning whirl

Before I realized what was happening
   My sons came along -- all three
Then I turned around again and
   They made a "grandmother" out of me

I thought things had settled down
   But another generation sprang up
And great grandkids kept on coming
   Like litters of little pups

However today I won't complain at all
   Because they're as cute as they can be
But I'm afraid before I turn around again
   A great-great grandmother I will be

08.12.07

Notation: As of July 2009, it happened! I did become a great-great grandmother. Then another one came in September 2010. What's next? Well, you might know, another one arrived in March 2012. Without a doubt, this poem must be dedicated to all of my current descendants and to more to come, maybe even before I get through publishing this book. Life is going by so fast. But, every day brings joy and more adventure into my life. Welcome to our world little Lilyanne, Joshua and Daniel; and an advance welcome to all of you yet to be born. Love, Great-Great Grandmother JoAnne

HELLO TO YOU, Little Joshua

H	It's not a special occasion
E	Nor is it a special season
L	Just wanted to say "Hello"
L	Who needs a "special" reason?
O	You are entering my life, so now
	All I am doing is -- just saying

Joshua, H E L L O

09.17.11

Dedicated to my first great-great grandson, Joshua Fairchild. (First child of my first great grandson, Benjamin Fairchild, who is the first child of my first granddaughter, Amy Holcomb Fairchild. Amy is the first daughter of my first son Donald Holcomb). You are from lots of firsts, little Joshua. (P .S I am the first child of my parents. too...And my mother is the first and only child of her parents.) Wow! Little Joshua you are really a Number One boy!

9

LIFE IS GOING BY SO FAST

Before this book I could complete
   A sweet little bundle just turned up
But because he is so very sweet
   I could never ever give him up

You slipped in right under the wire
   Oh you little rascal -- you
A cute little bundle I detect
   All dressed up in blue

Life just keeps on coming
   No matter what I do
Great-great grandchildren blooming
   Oh, but I'll love each one of you
03.30.12

Dedicated to Daniel Fairchild, #3 great-great. (He is the son of my great grandson, Benjamin Fairchild, who is the son of my granddaughter Amy, and Daniel is the grandchild of my #1 son, Donald). My legacy is gaining momentum. The longer I live, the greater I am.

THE SUMMER OF MY LIFE

Spring is the time of new beginnings
A time to look forward to what's ahead
The summer belongs to those in love
This is the summer of my life, it's said
     Now -- today

However the middle of summer's here for me
Still there's lots of life left for enduring love
I want a love that always will be true and kind
When fall comes, will stay and be my love
     'Til winter's end
07.10.78

Dedicated to the one I want to spend time with until winter's end,
my husband, Emery Tuttle -- my soul mate, my beloved.

ME

*"Who am I? Me. I'm myself. No other.
No duplicate. No clone. God created me,
and I'm who He wants me to be.
Nothing more. Nothing Less. Nothing else.
That's true for you, as well."*

(Quote: Luci Swindoll, <u>Joy</u> for <u>a</u> <u>Woman's</u> <u>Soul</u>, Barbara
Johnson, p. 9.)

JOB 12:12

"...Wisdom is with aged men,
With long life is understanding...."

I'M GETTING OLDER

I'm getting older
   Day after day after day
Now it is time for me
   To begin to change my way

No longer do I plan to be
   Just a prim and proper girl
I will try some different ways
   And give new things a whirl

Once I only dressed in black
   Or a little navy blue
But now I want bright, bright red
   And a little purple, too

I want to kick up my heels
   And dance and raise my hands
And do lots of witty things
   That no one understands

I'll go to amusing places
   Or maybe just go out to eat
Wearing bright purple dresses
   And red shoes upon my feet

Doting feathery red hats
   And dresses wild and gaudy
I'll do the thing that pleases me
   Even if it seems quite naughty
07.01.08

PATCHWORK LIVES

My life is like a patchwork quilt
Made from pieces of time sewn together
With stitches of laughter and tears
Each piece a different color and size
Depending upon the activities at hand
Some pieces are dark and dreary, but still
Are bordered by helping hands of friends

Pieces made by black and white events
At first bored me to tears; but were really okay
Because a friend was there beside me
Making the pieces fit into my patchwork life
Weaving all events into my life's story
Like the patchwork quilt, every piece is needed
To make it complete -- and beautiful -- and me
02.14.08

Notation: I am a quilter and I realize every piece is needed to give the finished product its value and purpose. This is true for our life as well. Every person and every event is needed to give our life its full value, color and purpose. I am grateful for all the pieces in my life, big and small, black and colored, new and old. Together they have made my life complete...and have defined me!

I WILL BE ME

If I did all the mischief
I just wanted to try
Before long rumors
Would surely start to fly

Then poems would be written so
Around the world could see
All the mischievous antics
That were done by me
08.01.80

13

YOU'RE ONLY AS OLD
As You Feel

You're only as old as you feel, they say
Well I feel like I'm 103 today
Yesterday it was a different thing
When I felt like twenty-three in spring

Overnight without even trying
I let the years go by flying
This phenomenon brings bewilderment
I don't know where those years all went

One day it will be in reverse -- you'll agree
And again I'll feel like I'm twenty-three
But I'm really glad I don't daily feel
Like I'm forty-three and over-the-hill!
06.24.78

Notation: I still feel 43 most days. Maybe I'll continue to feel 43 at least until, oops, my birthday August 1, 1978, when I turn 44!
I guess then that means, from that day forward, I'll be/feel over-the-hill!

JoAnne Thompson Holcomb Tuttle

Little me
Thompson

Then me
Holcomb

Now me
Tuttle

Future me???

"YOU'RE ONLY AS OLD AS YOU
FEEL"

MY REFLECTION

MY REFLECTION

Suddenly my reflection in the mirror
    Filled me with intense apprehension
A stirring breeze sent a chill across my soul
...As I stood for a moment mesmerized

As I gazed piercingly at that image
    Uneasiness permeated my heart
With a startling reminder of anxious years
    Of fearing this inevitable encounter

An unexpected calmness penetrated my fears
    As a burning desire to explore the unfamiliar
Drew me in for yet a closer look
    Then a quiet contentment prevailed

Quickly peacefulness filled my fretful heart
    I was drawn as though unto an old friend
Why was I so afraid for so many years; so
    Afraid to have this inevitable encounter?

I examined the reflection once again
    A pleasant feeling of detachment crept over me
As the reflection seemed to move in time
    I wondered...was what I saw real -- or not?

At first I saw in that reflection -- my youth
    Then I saw a frivolous, young woman -- me
Gay, light-hearted, free-spirited
    I smiled with great satisfaction; but then

A strange state of awareness suddenly emerged
    Something was missing -- there must be more
Once again the portrait changed before my eyes
    With each change new dimensions were added
Continued

I journeyed through this panorama of changes
   Watching more than half a century flash by
Youth -- maturity -- agedness...all three stages
   Each reflecting an undeniable thread of reality

The years truly had etched their paths
   Was it only the mark of the years I had feared?
But beauty can be found in every living thing
   No need to be afraid of passing time, I thought

In the silhouette of that reflection
   A certain radiance and glow appeared
Not beauty -- that is only skin deep
   But a gentle, genuine strength of character

Long years had forged this form as a blacksmith
   Forging fiery metal into usefulness
Suddenly, miraculously -- my struggle ceased
   The inflexible became flexible

What I once thought was a maze of
   Unspectacular, mundane or uneventful years
Now seemed quite provocative and challenging
   With a brilliant, peculiar charm all its own

Actually a startling phenomenon emerged; the
   Reflection portrayed a picture of contentment
Noting, many may *exist* until they are ninety --
   But very few really *live* past being twenty

A spontaneous second glance in the mirror
   Reflected back a stimulating realization
We only need to be afraid of aging and time
   If we haven't learned to *live* abundantly -- now

As I bid the reflection a*dieu*, I turned to ponder
   This wonder of man's intrinsic nature
Freed at last to continue my journey into
   The enchanted, mysterious realm of *tomorrow*
04.27.83

AGING BRINGS A NEW LOOK

No one ever told me
That when I finally do get old
No longer will I need to worry
I can let myself be *bold*

They didn't point out to feel *upbeat*
You make tired skin look alive
By just adding lots of make-up
Until finally you feel revived!

Nor did they mention there's a cocktail
Filled with gobs of vitamins and such
That's good for quickie energy-boosts
Although you might not like it much

They didn't predict the spirit of spring
Would rise up in my heart
Or say "don't settle for the predictable
But commence a brand new start"

No one advised me about *rediscovering*
Who and what I really want thus far
That if I venture into the vast unknown
I can hook my faded dreams upon a star
Continued

18

No one pointed out the rhapsodies missed
Because I didn't take "time" to hear
Nor mention it's time to discover that aging
Will bring a new look at things held dear

The deep blue sea, the sandy beach
The stars, the moon, the sun
These priceless things that were neglected
Because life was always "on-the-run"

Every inch of life is precious
I don't want to miss a single day
It's time to cultivate the extra-ordinary
With dramatic steps along the way

Aging brings me a *new look*
I won't' permit life to pass me by
Without taking time to smell the roses
'Cause that's an adventure worth a try
04.12.06

Notation: Don't forget to allow yourself to experience new things
every day. Don't miss a single adventure. Don't let life pass you
by.

MY LOVER
And My Best Friend As Well

I want someone -- a lover true
  Who's my best friend as well
Other loves in years gone past

Burned with hasty desire; but
  Could never blend two hearts to one
Only true love will grow and last

Sometimes it isn't clear to know
  That a gentle love can be desired
Then right before your eyes you find

That gentle love is growing
  You should open up your heart
If you find a love gentle and kind

If you discount or push gentle love aside
  Instead of allowing it time to grow
Abruptly that love could disappear

Life would become sad and lonely
  When you're alone the price is high
For no one's there to care or share

My dear, you have that gentle kind of love
  I want to open my heart to let it grow
If your gentle love is really true then

It will grow and be mine forevermore
  I want *you,* with your gentle love, to be
My *lover true as* well as my best friend
11.23.71

Dedicated to my true love, Emery, who is a man with a gentle
love; and I dedicated this poem to those who are able to love and
trust again.

JoAnne and Emery Tuttle

JoAnne Thompson Holcomb was married to Emery W. Tuttle on December 4, 1971.

Combined they have seven children (who now are grandparents). They have nineteen grandchildren, eighteen great grandchildren and three great-great grandchildren. That's a bunch.

They live in on Cedar Creek Lake, near a town called Gun Barrel City which is approximately seventy-five miles southeast of Dallas, Texas.

Both of them are retired but still lead a busy and exciting life. It's not over 'til it's over!

A PRIVATE AFFAIRE

The wind brushed leisurely
  Through my hair
Suddenly you were
  Standing there
I heard your jolly
  Friendly voice
I stood there quietly
  Devoid of choice

With certain qualities
  Hard to define
You made love-songs
  Come to my mind
You breezed in
  And buzzed about
You had charisma
  Without a doubt

As our eyes met
  In that crowded room
I knew then I had
  Met my doom
My eyes flashed back
  A puzzled glance
Was this meeting
  Just by chance?

A hint of irony
  In your smile
Told me you had been
  There for a while
I'm glad you were
  Just standing there
For that was the start
  Of our private affaire
02.02.81

THE QUARREL

I lie here an endless night
When you are mad at me
It seems that nighttime hurting
Is the worst form of agony

I guess that's why they said
On the day that we were wed
"Always make-up from a quarrel
Before you go to bed"

There is no consolation
That you lie there next to me
The fact that we're not speaking
Gives my pain intensity

We should just learn a lesson
And the next time that we fight
We should make-up very quickly
And not keep it through the night
02.09.72

EPHESIANS 4:32

*"...And be kind to one another
tenderhearted, forgiving each other
just as God in Christ also
has forgiven you..."*

NO MIGHT-HAVE-BEENS

If is an unreal word
It should be stricken from
   --All books
   --All words
   --All thoughts

There are no *ifs* or *might-have-beens*
Only what *is*-- and wishing won't change
   --Anything
   --Anyone
   --Anytime

What *if* things had not been as they were?
Would it have been good or bad?
   --For you?
   --For me?
   --For us?

Some things were very good -- some bad
I'm grateful for what we had
   --Everything
   --Good or
   --Bad

We only have now -- today
There are no *might-have-beens*
   --Not then
   --Not now
   --Not ever

Even so all we had and all we did together
Regardless, good or bad, makes us grow
   --In the past
   --In the present
   --In the future
07.09.78

I'M CAUGHT UP IN YOUR BEING

I can't forget your eyes
Alert, alive, alluring
So promising...

I listen for your voice
Soft, soothing, sensitive
So reassuring...

I reach out for your hand
Tempting, tender, touching
So caressing...

I seek your lips
Sweet, sensual, seductive
So provocative...

I cherish your love
Attentive, affectionate, adoring
So romantic...

I'm caught up in your being
Enticing, exciting, energizing
So vibrant...
09.28.71

Dedicated to my husband, Emery Tuttle. I'm caught up in the one
who stimulates me and makes me sparkle.

SEEDS

We planted tiny garden seeds
And watched our garden grow
We tilled the soil; then planted seeds
Watered, watched and pulled the weeds
   -- You and me
     -- Together

We had one tree so full of fruit
The branches nearly broke
Each night we dreamed soon we would be
Eating peaches from our tree
   -- You and me
     -- Together

Someone came while we were gone
They stole the peaches from our tree
You looked again, all you could see
Was just one peach left on our tree
   -- One for you and me
     -- Together

By candle light that night we ate
One single precious peach
I took a bite, then gave you one
Sharing it was so much fun
   -- For you and me
     -- Together
Continued

26

Daily looking out our garden window
Watching as you labored
Love-seeds quietly started seeping
Into my heart were gently creeping
   -- Binding you and me
     -- Together

Tilling, planting, weeding often
Will help a garden grow
We should remember not to fail
To treat our love-seeds just as well
   -- Keeping you and me
     -- Together

Again the soil is warm and ready
It is time to plant the seeds
Working side-by-side let's also start
Planting more love-seeds in our heart
   -- Solidifying you and me
     -- Together
06.15.72

Dedicated to the first year of our marriage when we planted our first vegetable garden together and we grew in our ability to work together and enjoy the fruits of our labor. Our love grew and we became as one, bound together by growing love. This poem is based on a true happening when someone did steal all of our peaches except one from our little tree while we were gone...but, it did not stop the joy we had sharing one precious peach -- together.

THOUGHTS OF YOU

I peeled an orange today
  and thought of you
A funny thing to do
  to make me think of you

I miss this simple thing
  so thoughts of you
Came running through my mind
  as sometimes thoughts will do

I ate one little slice
  then thought of you
I did not have you near
  to share a slice with you

A slice of orange for me
  a slice for you
I peeled an orange each night
  and shared a slice with you

Funny how this simple thing
  makes me feel so sad
An orange just for myself
  you'd think would make me glad
Continued

28

To give one bite to you
   then take a bite for me
Made every bite we took
   as sweet as it could be

I have another orange
   it's so round and smooth
I'd like to peel that orange
   and share a slice with you

I'd like to share my orange
   but now that you are gone
It surely is no fun at all
   to eat my orange alone

That's why eating oranges
   brings me thoughts of you
There's really no one else I want
   to share my orange -- but you!
11.12.72

Dedicated to my husband, Emery, the one with whom I love to share all of my life. As it sometimes happens, the newly married go through some rough patches, but true love wins out. We patched our rough patches.

DREAMS

Off to sleep with tender thoughts
   Glowing warmly in my head
In a half-dream, midnight haze
   Aimlessly those thoughts spread

Nature spins her golden thread
   Making cobwebs in my mind
Peace I had not hoped to gain
   Floating there for me to find

Suddenly from far away
   In the stillness of the night
All the things I wanted most
   Now were mine until daylight

Who would dare seek refuge now?
   Without trust the spell would break
Beyond the bounds of life there lies
   Magic mine alone to take

Shinning moon and swelling seas
   Music, laughter, sun-kissed sand
Love abounding, waiting there
   Reaching up to take my hand

Continued

Captured by the grasp of it
    Daring not to comprehend
Hidden meanings burning low
    Lest the dream come to an end

Slipping deeper into paradise
    Penetrating into the past
Visualizing perfect love
    Which evermore would last

Soon the moon drifts slowly on
    Leaving with its warm embrace
Stealing quietly through the sky
    Moving on without a trace

Quietly as the dawn breaks through
    Spare me waking with a start
Night has cast its magic spell
    Dreams of you rest in my heart
03.04.78

Dedicated to my husband as are most of my love poems.
He is my soul mate, true love and the one who brings sweet
dreams into my night.

WHAT'S HAPPENING?

Something's different about me
Puzzling you see
Suddenly without my knowing
Poems have started flowing

Things are so exciting
That I have started writing
So poems I shall bestow
On all the friends I know

Each time I start to speak
A poem from me will leak
It seems now all the time
I only "*think*" in rhyme

Now what is even worse
I even "*dream*" in verse
What's happening?
What's happening?
06.13.78

ATTITUDE CORRECTION

Wishing you a better
Birthday attitude
Remember
You're Not getting Older...
You're Just getting...
BETTER!

So be Happy
On your Happy Birthday
02.12.10

WANNA-BEES

"Wanna-bees" are everywhere
   Ideas flying rampant
   Pen or pencil in their hand
Writing without a word to spare

Is their story truth or fiction?
   As their plot grows lofty, a tale is spun
   Upbeat, downbeat -- a web woven
Unfolding mystery and a little action

Will the characters love or hate?
   Every character's role's must be divulged
   A beautiful girl -- the handsome man
But only the end will reveal their fate

Last page's written – the book's complete
   But there's one thought missing
   Squeeze it in -- now it's done!
But this new notion's not discreet!

In Chapter One -- he was her brother!
   Whoa!.....they *can never* fall in love!
   Another scheme we must find
Erase that plot and write another

That didn't work -- let's start again
   But gee wiz – I thought it sounded good
   But now we must write another scene
To bring this saga to an end
05.29.06

Notation: I'm also a "wanna-be," so I dedicate this poem to myself and all other "wanna-be" poets and authors. I want to thank the members of the Dallas Writers Group for their encouragement and counsel, and I wish each of them success in their own endeavors...publish, publish, publish!

LONGFELLOW
I Must Have Been Misnamed

I'm sure when I was born
I was given the wrong name
If I had been called "Longfellow"
By now I would have fame

My poems are just as good
As any that are his
I'm sure it's just his "*name*"
That got him in this "*biz*"

Throughout my entire life
My friends would always say
"I know you will surely be
A famous poet some day"

"The reason that we know it is"
All of them would bellow
"Your big feet really show it -- so
You should be called *Longfellow*"

Therefore fate has turned on me
And took my fame away
Had my name been changed at birth
I would be rich today

---A *"Wanna-be Poet"*

08.15.78

34

HAPPY RED HAT DAY

Where is my big **red hat?**
Where is my purple dress?
I need to go right now
But my hair is such a mess

I need another bracelet
Maybe a ring or two
I must dress up real pretty
To keep up with all of you

Purple dresses -- big red hats
We'll go out to eat and play
Heads will turn, eyes will glare
To see us dressed that way

People think we're funny
And just a little strange
And maybe should be locked up
Because we act deranged

I'm a little **Red Hat** Lady
And really glad to be
With other **Red Hat** Ladies
Who look and act like me

Happy **Red Hat** Day!
07.11.08

RED HAT BIRTHDAYS
Are in Style

Well *Red Hat* Birthdays
Are always in style
We dress up weirdly
And make people smile

We sing Happy Birthday
Perhaps out of tune
We eat cake and ice cream
'Til we have no more room

Bright purple and red hats
We're striking in style
And everyone keeps hoping
We'll be gone in a while

Don't be dismayed
Don't be alarmed
Whatever we do
We first do no harm

We're old, as you know
Just watch what we do
Then wait and one day
It will surely be *you!*
08.01.08

Notation: This is the year of my 74th birthday and I am a Red Hat Lady named Pretty Princess JoAnne (named by my loving husband, Emery).So, put on a **red hat** and join me, if you dare!

TRASH TO TREASURES

I love trash
To me it's treasure
Changing its nature
Gives me great pleasure

Angels or snowmen
Made from a bottle
Small scraps of wood
Carved into a model

Beautiful quilts
From little cloth pieces
Painting old rocks
To be animal species

Bunnies or kittens
A doll for a child
Or something to put
On a shelf for a while

Seashells or pinecones
Become new creations
Glitter and bows
Make them real sensations

Don't throw away
That trash in your attic
Give it to me
I am a real "trash" addict

I see a treasure
In stuff in your trunk
I'll create new things
From all of your junk
03.24.06

Dedicated to one of my favorite pastimes, making "treasures out of trash" and to all scrap-crafters and trash-collectors who enjoy the same.

MY ATTIC IS FULL

What shall I do
With all this stuff?
When will I ever
Have just enough?

Chairs and lamps
And all kinds of vases
Pictures and pottery
From all kinds of places

An old rocking horse
With only one leg
A fancy wine goblet
An empty beer keg

The attic is full
The basement is stacked
OOPS -- one more thing
My closet just cracked!

What shall I choose
To just give away?
Oh, I can't do that
Might need it someday!

What shall I do
With all of these things?
My dresser is full
Of bracelets and rings
Continued

When I go a strolling
Down to the mall
I see lots of things
I don't need at all

How can I stop
Getting this stuff?
Will I ever learn
Enough is enough?

What shall I do
With all of my stuff?
I'll give it to you
Then you'll have *enough!*

Addendum:
   This is my revised version of the last verse that was influenced
by Kimyla Guice Stegall. It doesn't mean I agree with her
philosophy on the value of "trash."

What will she do
With all of her stuff?
She'll **sell** it to you
And still have enough!
03.20.06

Dedicated to and inspired by my writer friend Kimyla Guice
Stegall and her book, "The Cash Cow." Kimyla endorses *"sell"*
not "**keep** junk." But, that doesn't stop us from being friends.

MY ATTIC IS CLEAN

My attic is clean
　My pockets are full
I sold that old stuff
　That's my new rule

I'll let someone else
　Collect for a while
Then I'll be richer
　High stepping in style
04.24.06

Dedicated to Kimyla Guice Stegall, my writer friend and author of "The Cash Cow," a book about getting rid of all your junk. I take the "fifth "and will not admit to whether or not I have actually read her book; after all, I am an admitted junk-collector -- addict, that is...guilty as charged, I don't know how this poem managed to invade my poetic thoughts.

MATTHEW 6:21

"...For where your treasure is there will your heart be also..."

Notation: I want my treasure to be with God in Heaven and I want yours to be there, too. However, all my junk is in the attic! (sic)

A GET WELL MESSAGE

I heard you are sick
This get well card and with it too
Come special wishes
Just for you

I hope that you will improve
More and more each new day
And soon you'll be well enough
To be up and going right away
10.15.04

A GET WELL WISH
FOR YOU

A get well wish for you
Sincerely hoping
very, very soon

You will be feeling
Much, much better
Back in perfect tune
10.15.04

BREAK THE HOLY BREAD

Break the Holy Bread
Share His precious cup
It's the promise of His presence
And His perfect love
04.15.83

1 CORINTHIANS 11:26

"...For as often as you eat this bread
Or drink this cup,
you proclaim the Lord's death
'till He comes..."

JOHN 3:16

"For God so loved the world,
that He gave His only begotten Son, that
whosoever believeth in Him should not perish
but have everlasting life"

LET MY LIFE SING

Let my life sing
With perfect trust
Let it sing loudest
When I share love

Let my life sing
Each day that goes by
Let it sing in the morning
And continue through night

Let my life sing
In the midst of rough times
Let my life sing
Transforming tears into smiles

Let my life sing
It's contagious, my friend
Come catch my song
And let your life sing

Let your life sing
With God's perfect trust
Then let your life sing
So others will know
03.24.06

HE LIFTED MY SOUL
(Song)

He washed me
He cleansed me
He gave me His love
He lifted my soul to His own

He gave me
Such joy when
He wrapped me in love
And offered to make me His own

He sent me
His Spirit
His promise to pledge
Never to leave me alone

He washed me
He cleansed me
He gave me His love
He lifted my soul to His own
01.16.83

Notation: Written on the occasion of my baptism in the Holy Spirit at The Church of the Resurrection, Dallas, Texas, when the Holy Spirit inspired this song in tongues; then He gave me the interpretation of the tongues, as well as providing the tune for the song   by   His   Spirit.

HOLY, HOLY, HOLY
(Song)

Holy, Holy, Holy, Holy
Holy is the name of my Lord

Holy, Holy, Holy, Holy
Holy is the name of my Lord

He's the Rock of my Salvation
He's my Cornerstone
My faith's on His Foundation
Holy is the name of my Lord

Holy, Holy, Holy, Holy
Holy is the name of my Lord

Holy, Holy, Holy, Holy
Holy is the name of my Lord
04.04.88

Dedicated to the inspiration of the Holy Spirit in my life. The most important thing in my life is my relationship with my Lord and Savior Jesus Christ who extends to everyone eternal life.

ISAIAH 6:3

"...Holy, Holy, Holy is
the Lord of hosts; the whole
earth is full of His glory..."

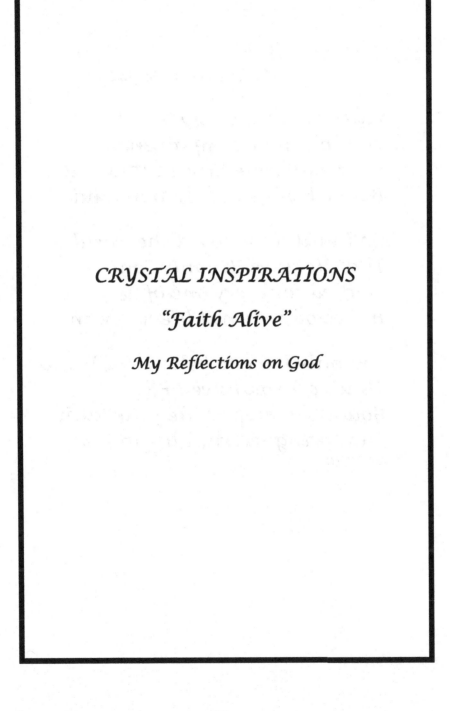

CRYSTAL INSPIRATIONS

"Faith Alive"

My Reflections on God

FAITH ALIVE
My Reflections on God

Faith is not an easy thing
To explain or comprehend
Every man one day must face it
Before his life draws to an end

God said He so loved the world
That He gave His only Son
To died for every one of us
Hence our eternal life was won

You only have to believe His Word
That's all you have to do
God will even provide your faith
That brings eternal life to you
07.27.10

HOLY SPIRIT,
Breathe on Me

The leaves fall for
Every wind that blows
They drift along
Wherever that wind goes

We only need to yield
To God's gentle breath
All other surging winds
Will only bring us death

Ever ready may I be
For God's breath to blow on me
Holy Spirit, 'tis my plea
Holy Spirit, breathe on me

From whence it comes
I do not know
Only with you, Lord
Will I gladly go...

Holy Spirit, Breathe on Me
04.18.83

GOD'S LOVE

Without God's love
My life would be
As empty as
Any life could be

God gives unmerited
Love to me -- and you
Forever...never failing love
Agape love...pure and true

God cares for me -- and you
As no other ever can
God's Savior gave His life
For each and every man

Receive His love
And you will be
Forever with Him
Through all eternity
02.14.09

GOD REJOICES

Christ died for us that we might live
His gift was given for our sake
There's nothing you must do or pay
His gift is there for you to take

God delights with immense joy
When one lost sinner is redeemed
Because forever that sinner's spirit
Is locked into our God Supreme
02.22.09

IT IS FINISHED

"It is finished," said the Master
"It is finished on the Cross..."
"I have paid the price forever
To redeem mankind who's lost"

Jesus paid the price for you, and
That same price He paid for me
The ultimate price paid forevermore
From that Cross on Calvary

As Jesus died upon the Cross
What He said for me -- and you
Was, "Father, please forgive them
For they know not what they do"

But His death was not **His** finish
Because victory was His alone
He burst forth from the grip of *Death*
To shout the *Victor's* song

For you and me -- it **is** finished
By that Cross on Calvary
When we put our trust in Jesus
We have Christ's gift -- *eternity*
02.06.87

HAVE YOUR WAY WITH ME

When I try to mold you, Lord
Into a form to suit myself
Or when I try to tell you, Lord
Just hide my sins upon the shelf

Sorrow fills your tender eyes
Because patiently you have loved me
You've already paid the price and
From all my sins you've set me free

Please have your way with me, Lord
Take my life and let it be
Pleasing in your sight, Lord
Because you died for me!
10.10.83

THE RANSOM PRICE

The Holy One of Israel
Was sent by God to earth
He brought with Him His Majesty
Hidden by His lowly birth

He came to pay the ransom price
To set the captives free
It took His death to pay that price
That God required for me.
09.03.00

JESUS DIED FOR YOU

May this Easter season
Make you totally aware
That Jesus died for you
Because for you he cared

Jesus is God's only Son
Given that you'll be saved
So you can have eternal life
Because *your* sins He waived

Ask Him into your heart
And always He'll be there
Because God so loved you
That your life He freely spared
10.09.08

Dedicated to the most important celebration we have, Easter Sunday...the celebration of the resurrection of our Savior, Jesus Christ our Lord.

GOD'S LOVE IS FREE

God's love is free and unconditional
It's neither deserved, nor is it earned
God's precious love is freely given
To us by His initiative alone

The promise of God's love
Has been given to every man
A love irrevocable and unchangeable
So we can rest in what Christ did

God gave His Son to be the Sacrifice
It was the perfect price
Sufficient to fulfill God's perfect law
And purchase back my life

God looked beyond the circumstances
That ripped and tore my life
Actively working on my behalf
God bestowed abundant Grace
Continued

All my old and tainted man
Was changed in just an instant
When God's righteousness triumphed
Through Jesus Christ, His perfect Son

I was resurrected from the dead
By Jesus' life and death
When He arose up from the grave
Eternal life to me was granted

Now I have abundant, overflowing life
Which Jesus gave so freely
I shall reign with Him forever
Because of God's unconditional love for me

Christ the perfect, unblemished Lamb
Paid the highest price of all
I can't repay Him for what He did
To redeem a wretch like me
09.04.01

HEAR MY PRAYER, O LORD

I want to know You, Lord

Hear my prayer, O Lord
Answer me quickly
Don't keep me suspended, but
Comprehend my deep, agonizing pain

Be not indifferent to my needs
For they are great
When you don't answer me
I feel totally alone -- abandoned

I am made ashamed before my enemies
That I cannot testify of your favor
I think you don't care
And then I am disheartened

Yet you, O Lord God of Israel, you alone
Were ever there and ever mindful of me
You marked my paths before I knew you
You waited upon me and loved me

Even when I transgressed against you
With patience and mercy
You waited all the day long
You were always near me

When I was desolate and afflicted
You brought forth your mercy
You redeemed me with everlasting love
And you established my steps

Although I have not innocent hands
And my eye wanders away from you
Still you bathe me in your love and
Dress me in *your* righteousness
Continued

56

You teach my heart and guide me
In the steps of your song, and you
Fill my cup with your love and
The blood of your body

Why do I still not *know, really know* your face?
The question was too hard, so I set it by
But now, O Lord, my God
I need to know your Name -- to know *you*

I need to see you face to face
Don't leave me or forsake me now
For there is no other Name
Whereby I am saved

Who are you, my God, my Lord?
I want to *know you...really know you*
I am weak, Lord, and weary
Filled with my own grief

I gave no remembrance to Thee, but
Turned unto my own understanding
Yet you were and were patient
Gentle beyond all reason

You let me stretch out far from Thee
But you did not destroy me
Nor let me fall in my transgression
Instead you became a shield about me

A fortress to receive this wayward passerby
You drew me out of that self-made mire
And set my head high
You have dealt graciously with me
Continued

Diligent to deliver me
And design my path
You encompassed me with your love
Until I am restored

You are the One who
From everlasting to everlasting
Searches for that lost one -- *me*
Until all restitution is complete

Praise be to the Name of my Lord
Who cares for me
Many times I've heard you speak, my Lord
But paid you no mind

For I was waiting for you
To speak as Thunder
For I know you are a mighty God, who with
A word can break the cedars of Lebanon

You are a mighty and strong God
You are full of majesty
I am waiting for you to reveal yourself to me
By that power which shakes me to my bones

But when you spoke, you spoke to me
Like quiet, deep waters
So I paid You no heed
I gave no ear to that faint whisper

It was so near to silence
It did not make my bones quake
Consider my frailty, O Lord, and
Forgive my faithlessness
Continued

Do not withhold even Thy breath from me
I won't turn my ear from Thee again
Nor will I doubt Thy faithfulness
Neither Thy majesty, nor Thy power anymore

For when you whisper, O Lord, my God
It does thunder across the valleys
Your voice does roar upon the mountains
Yet it is truly only a whisper and life is created

You are the great "I Am"
You are everything
That is or was or ever will be
How can I fail to see who you are?

How can I fail to trust who you are?
How can I not know *you?*
When I mourn, you are Comfort
When I falter, you are Strength

When I am sick, you are Healer
When I am weak, you are Strong
All that I am not, you Are – you are Everything
All that I have not, you Have – have Everything

All that I want, you Give
All that I need, you Supply
You never change -- everlasting to everlasting
You stay the same

It is I who vacillates and falters
Turning from straw to straw for help
Even the Heavens know who you are
And declare your Glory
Continued

I indeed recognize who you are
You are the great "I Am"
I want to passionately praise you, Lord
And I want to unfathomably know **You**

To give you praise which is acceptable
And joyous to your ear because I *know* you
I want to exalt you above the gifts
You have given me

To praise you for your excellence alone
Your gifts are bountiful without number
Your gifts are excellent beyond compare
What praise would be worthy of your glory

What praise would have favor
In your sight, O great Jehovah
You are to be praised by my willing heart
You are to be honored by my total obedience

You are to be glorified
By my unwavering faithfulness
You are worthy to be praised by the Heavens
And praised in all the earth

You are worthy of my faithfulness
Yet there is no faithfulness in me
Neither obedience nor willing heart
Unless **You** provide it for me

When I know you, Lord
I will taste of your honeycomb, Lord
Your sweetness will linger on my lips
Into the darkness of the dreariest night
Continued

60

When I know you, Lord
I will know your sweetness fully
When I truly know you, Lord
I will taste the bitterness of your pain

When my sin is set before you
When I know you, Lord
Then and only then will my sin
Become bitterness to me, too

When I know you, Lord
I will walk the length of your path
I will not falter
Nor become weary

When I know you, Lord
My steps will be numbered by your hand
The length and breadth and depth
Will all be yours

When I know you, Lord
Really know you, Lord
There will be no limits -- no time
Nor lack of time...I will be totally yours

We will be as one
When I know you, Lord
I will be no more, but I will become
But that only happens -- is only possible

When I really know you, Lord
Help me to **know You, Lord** that way
Then I will be all you want for me
Only you are worthy; for you are truly God
Continued

Then, and only then, I will be no more
But will be dead to self and belong to you
Then and only then will I be able
To know and truly exalt you, my God, my Lord
Amen
10.17.86

Notation: My meditation during a Christian Women's Retreat. With the Church of the Resurrection, Dallas, Texas, November 1986.

PSALM 46:10

"...Cease striving and know that I am God;
I will be exalted among the nations,
I will be exalted in the earth..."

LET ME HEAR YOUR VOICE, LORD

Whisper softly in my ear, Lord
Gently tug my broken heart
Let me hear your gentle voice
To reflect on what you impart

Give me unwavering faith, Lord
In your goodness from above
Let me savor your Holy presence
Know your mercy and your love
10.17.83

SOUNDS FROM SILENCE

I seek a place to refresh my senses
Far away from the work-a-day world
A refuge in God's great outdoors
Where diverse living things dwell

Greeting the dawn of each new day
Reaching their zenith with God's blessings
The untamed bids me to stand in awe
Of God's great created wonders

In the silence of this sanctuary
I can hear most audibly the sound
Of God's thundering voice
Resounding deep within my soul

When all else around me
Stands empty void and silent
The voice of God can penetrate
That silence and fill my emptiness
10.02.82

HE IS RISEN

Overcoming death, victory is complete
　　There's nothing left to fear
Christ gave His life and conquered sin
　　He wiped away each tear

Arise from all the bonds of earth
　　Distrust, despair and fear
Arise to beauty, love and joy
　　For His sweet peace is here

Count all other things but loss
　　Then all fears will disappear
For naught can ever do you harm
　　Rest assured for Christ is near

He is risen -- His victory is complete
　　There's nothing for us to fear
He paid our price; He bought us back
　　Because He held us dear
10.18.83

MY QUESTION:

Have you ever walked on a twilight eve
　　And listened to a katydid's song...
When the peace of God rests upon the earth and
　　The fragrance of praise awaits those who long?

Participating in God's marvelous wonders
　　Will put a smile upon your face
As you listen to the katydid's song
　　You will hear praise for God in His Holy Place
01.16.10

GOD BREATHED ON ME

My tiny, broken spirit
   Lay there limp and lifeless
Until God breathed on me
   And filled me with His likeness

I didn't have enough faith to believe
   Not an iota of what I would need
But His Spirit sent His faith to me
   The size of a grain of mustard seed

That tiny, little seed of faith did start
   To penetrated my hardened heart
Exactly enough to permit God in my heart
   So the Holy Spirit's work could start

God's Holy Spirit breathed on me
   Allowing His miraculous work to proceed
From faith the size of a mustard seed
   With Jesus in my heart my pain's relieved
01.14.83

Dedicated to the occasion of my baptism in the Holy Spirit at
The Church of the Resurrection, Dallas, Texas, 1983.

MATTHEW 17:20

"...Because of the littleness of your faith;
for truly I say to you,
if you have faith as a mustard seed,
you shall say to this mountain,
'Move from here to there,'
and it shall move; and
nothing shall be impossible to you..."

PRAISE YOUR HOLY NAME

Dear God, you are our God, our all
　Why don't we always upon your Name call?
You'd cheerfully meet our every need
　And come when called with perfect speed

Dear God, you have the ideal plan
　But we might not fully understand
Our life is in your special keeping
　You care and that is what we're seeking

O God, you're our help in every need
　Why don't we ever let you lead?
You've been faithful in all you've done
　You keep your word to everyone

I now release my life to you
　Your will be done in all I do
May I always walk and talk and stand
　And through life with you go hand-in-hand

Thank you, dear God, you hear my plea
　Thank you, dear God, you care for me
Through all of time you remain the same
　Praise you, dear God, Praise your Holy Name
04.24.83

PRAISE YOUR NAME, O LORD

Praise your Name, O Lord
Praise your Holy Name
You are ever with me, O Lord

Have been with me always
Even in the shadow of death
You were with me

In the midst of my enemies
When I was afraid or forlorn
You were with me

When I was the prodigal son
Your patience endured forever
You were with me

When I turned my back on you
Your tolerance quietly waited
You were with me

You have loved me unconditionally
And your unmerited love is eternal
Praise your Holy Name for you are with me
03.01.08

THE KEY

Go deep into God's very presence
Relinquish each moment as you go
Ascend beyond your highest hopes
To the deepest love you'll ever know

The key that unlocks that door
Is very simple -- you just obey
No blessing will He deny you
Nor any promise keep away

Dwell not upon what is past
Lest His Sacrifice is vain
He'll turn your mourning into joy
Releasing you from all your pain
10.17.83

AN INTERIOR DESIGN

An interior design
Is what I have in mind
Something deep inside me
True beauty for you to find

Built one stone upon another
But with softness all around
The softness that exposes
Where God's agape love is found
09.30.01

THE BRIDGE

Our God and our Lord
We joy in Thy presence
Fear would fill our hearts
Without your precious essence

The light from your existence
Is flung across the years
It's radiance prepares the way
So our hearts will have no fears

God is the bridge -- the path
From the unknown into the known
If we follow in His footsteps
We will never walk alone
01.05.84

A HAPPY FACE

A happy face
Has its place
In the midst
Of God's creation

Happy smiles
Travel miles
To bring God's love
To every nation
09.11.85

REFLECTIONS

I noticed radiance
A special glow
Shining softly before me

I observed a cheerful smile
And peaceful spirit
Spreading joy around me

I discerned a gentle nature
A loving kindness
Flowing quietly toward me

I perceived penetrating love
With such refreshing beauty
Reflecting **"living"** Christianity to me
10.08.82

LIFE'S MOMENTS

Life's moments should be
A series of joyous
Live-to-the-fullest
Unexpected moments

Life's moments should keep us
Serene and confident and
Triumphantly vital by truly
Enhancing our very being
09.28.72

70

I LIFT YOU UP IN PRAYER
Today

I lift you up in prayer today
   May God bless you in every way
I ask Him for a peaceful day
   And all the love He can display

He'll let you know He's ever there
   And show you all His tender care
He'll shower blessings in abundant share
   And a single joy He will not spare

He'll teach you how to understand
   He has a strong and willing hand
To neither judge nor reprimand
   But just to love you where you stand

I lift you up in prayer each day
   That God will show you His perfect way
Set aside your own prayer time today
   For Him to guide you all the way
05.03.83

PHILIPPIANS 4:6

"...Be anxious for nothing,
but in everything
by prayer and supplication,
with thanksgiving
let your requests be made known
to God..."

HOUSE BLESSING PRAYER

May God richly bless your home
   and every person in it
May the Cross and all it stands for
   be the center of all that's in it

May God the Father, Son and Spirit
   throughout this household reign
Let this family be ruled by love
   and forever praise God's Name

May God's love fill every area
   of this home and each one's heart
May God's richest, fullest blessing
   upon this home now start
09.14.83

MAY THE SPIRIT OF THE LORD
Rest Upon You

May the Spirit of God rest upon you
As we celebrate the day of your birth
For God sent His Holy Spirit
To all His children here on earth

May His Holy Spirit strengthen you
And give you love beyond compare
May you always seek God's presence
And know that He is there

As each passing year goes by
May you grow deeper in the Lord
May all God's promises be granted you
According to His Word

LET US CELEBRATE
YOUR HAPPY, HAPPY BIRTHDAY
07.07.74

A SONG FOR MATTHEW
(A song)

I bind that Spirit of Fear in you
I bind it back; I bind it back
I bind that Spirit of Fear in you
And cast it out like Christ would do

I bind it back, and cast it out
I cast it out in Jesus' name
I bind that Spirit of Fear in you
And cast it out like Christ would do

Let God's Spirit of Peace and Love
Fill you up; fill you up
Let God surround you with His love
And send His Peace down from above
05.05.86

Dedicated to Matthew. A song for Matthew who was born with
cerebral palsy. God inspired a song that calmed him when he
wouldn't stop crying. Whenever I sang this song to him, he would
drop off to sleep peacefully. God's Spirit is our Comforter.

SIGNS AND SYMBOLS

We use special signs and symbols
   For things we all hold dear
The heart a symbol of our love
   A dove shows peace is here
Certain symbols denote winter
   Others show that spring is near

We can use almost anything
   The moon, a star, the sun
To represent our deepest thoughts
   Or pledge sacred vows to someone
A circle means unending love
The cross tells us what was done

Our understanding is illuminated
   By the little cloverleaf
For it portrays the relationship
   Of the blessed Trinity's motif
The Father, Spirit, Son -- are *Three...but*
   Just **One God** -- our indefinable ***belief***
08.11.83

THIS LITTLE CLOVERLEAF

This little cloverleaf
    Is symbolic of our belief
    Showing the Father, Spirit, Son
    All Three -- yet shows our God is only **One**

We can never understand
    For we're only mortal man
    Our "One God" is a "Trinity"
    Who is and was and always will be

We can't separate His parts
    Nor explain Him in our hearts
    God's all Three -- Father, Son and Spirit
    To know He's only *ONE*...only faith can hear it
03.11.83

Notation: This poem was written for one of many greeting cards that were taken to Silver Leaves Nursing Home as part of the Outreach Ministry of The Church of the Resurrection, Dallas, Texas.

MY
LOVE POEMS

LOVE is so contagious...
It can pass from one unto another
Until every man in every nation
Becomes our Christian brother

LOVE is quite infectious...
A little hug passed to one another
Will soon be caught by the entire world
'Til every man's our brother

LOVE of Christ in your daily life...
Will brighten every day
Taking all cold and bitterness away
We will love others in the Christian way

The LOVE of God abides...
We can give our LOVE to one another
Because God's LOVE is unmerited for all
His agape LOVE is for every brother

God's agape LOVE means...
I am His and so are others
His agape LOVE will help me
Make all men my brothers

In LOVE, An impromptu smile...
Will quicken the start of a spark
That will spread God's LOVE
Into every person's heart
01.15.83

LET GOD'S SUNSHINE IN

Let God's sunshine
Pour into your life
Fill you with His mercy
Protect you from all strife

Let God's sunshine
Wrap you like a hug
Shower you with goodness
Keep you warm and snug

Let God's sunshine
Lift your heart up high
Fill you with His power
Reveal to you He's nigh

Let God's sunshine
Open up the door
Manifest His wonders
Show His glory evermore
08.01.83

ENDLESS CIRCLE

Let the Spirit of
God's love
Flow from God,
to you, to others
There will be
an endless circle
As we all love
one another
10.02.83

BURDENS ARE HEAVY

When your burdens get too heavy
And you don't know what to do
Imagine you're a little rock
Then this is what you'll do

Pretend you are that little rock
Just a sittin' on a hill
You never have to do a thing
But just sit still

You never eat; you never sleep
You never even wash
You just sit there a thousand years
And rest yourself by gosh

Your Heavenly Father then takes over
To do things you can't see
He never eats; He never sleeps
'Cause He's answering your plea
03.03.02

OUR BURDEN-BEARER

Christ, our Lord, our Friend
All our burdens you will bear
We only daily have to carry
A teeny, weenie, little share

Lead us in all truth
Redeem us when we fall
Shield and protect us
Have mercy on us all

Hold us in your hand
Guide us day by day
Let us rest in you
Along this perilous way

Christ, our Lord, our Friend
There is no one who is fairer
A countless, thousand times
You are our Burden-Bearer
01.05.84

JAMES 5:14

"Is there any sick among you?
Let him call for the elders
of the church;
and let them pray over him,
anointing him with oil
in the name of the Lord"
Amen

GET WELL WISHES

I'm sending you a bouquet
Of prayers and get well wishes
To speed up your recovery
And put you back
The way you ought to be!
10.15.04

A GET WELL PRAYER

May God be there beside you
To comfort, heal and guide you
May God keep you on the pathway
Of health and joyfulness today

My prayer and blessing for you
is
Get *well* soon
10.15.04

GET WELL QUICK

It's great to see you
Up and about
It made me want to
Sing and shout

"Thank you Lord for
Answered prayer
Thank you Lord for
Being there"

I'm sending genuine
Concern for you
And hope in time
You're good as new

I'll always continue
To pray for you
And I'm sending love
And blessings, too

Notation: Another one of my hobbies is to write the verses and make my own greeting cards. I'm a scrap-crafter and I make my greeting cards out of re-cycled material. These cards are usually personalized to the occasion and person. Included in this collection are a few examples of my greeting card verses. All of them put together would be another book.

DROP YOUR REQUEST IN GOD'S MAILBOX
He Always Delivers

Let go so God can take over
For Him there's nothing
Too great or
Too small

Relinquish, release and then rest
Give all the results to Him
Our Redeemer
Our All

See God through the eyes of faith
Find a fresh revelation of Him
Our Savior
Our All

Just let go so God can take over
For Him there's nothing
Too great or
Too small

He will deliver and keep us
That's who He is -- He is
Our Deliverer
Our All
08.01.83

A CHRISTIAN WITNESS

She touched my life
Just slightly so
But with that touch
I was to know
A woman filled
With tender love
And hope and faith
From God above
Her touch will linger
Although she would go
I'll always remember
Her Christian glow
03.27.80

NOTATION: We need to be aware that we don't always know who is watching us or how our witness might affect the life of the person watching us. The way we live our life before others may be the only Christian testimony that person sees or remembers. The person who inspired this poem never knew how her Christian life touched my life. This poem was written reflecting upon her life and how I remembered her.

MY COMFORTER

I ache, but...
How do I cope with despair and pain?
If I hide it, disguise it, or bury it deep inside
　Will it stop?
　Will it disappear?

I search, but...
Where is my relief? Where is my comfort?
When I seek relief, it disappears like cotton-candy
　No relief is found
　No comfort comes

The ache continues...
When will the thrashing inside me stop?
It persistently stings; burning with a driving pain
　It's part of me
　But I want no part of it

All my efforts fail...
All I try with all my might and strength fails
Nothing is enough; everything is inadequate
　Availing me naught
　Failing me completely

But when I yield it all to you, O Lord...
By your Spirit, you remove all my pain
Your love reaches down to touch my aching heart
　Only then, by you am I relieved
　Only then, by you am I comforted
11.13.83

MY FRIEND

My Lord, my God, my Friend
Let me joy in Thee
My fretful heart unafraid
When you walk with me

Stand between the years with me
Reach back into my past
Hold me close right now to Thee
Cover the future, 'er so vast

Your radiance flows across the days
Your warmth lasts through the night
You swallow up my soul's deep pain
And fill me with true delight

This world's cruelness left behind
My trust I'll place in you
The one who wipes away my tears
And gives me life anew

You're always there to guide me
Not one step shall I take alone
When I'm filled with your precious joy
All the bitterness is gone

You lift my soul to heights untold
Out of the depths of pain and sin
You renew my strength, my joy, my life
Faithful, constant...you're my Friend
10.13.83

MAGICAL MOMENTS

We wish you a Christmas season
Filled with the magical moments
That God provides for all those
Who love Him and believe
His Son, Jesus Christ, is Lord
02.24.09

THE JOY OF CHRIST'S LOVE

The joy of Christ's love
brightens each day
He will take all cold
and bitterness away...

The love of Christ abides
'til the end of time
because I am His
and He is truly mine...

Love...to you...for you
...from you
...to others...for others
...from others...to you...is

An endless circle of God's love
A love that's truly
for you and me
from Christ's Divine Love
02.14.83

NEWS-WORTHY TALK

Spread the news about the Father
How He sent His only Son
Spread the news about Christ Jesus
Why He died upon the Cross
Spread the news about the Spirit
When He filled you with His power
Spread the news about God's kingdom
Where eternal life is found

Talk all you want to everyone about
What God has done for you
Talk all you want about the Good News
The Good News of God's redemptive power
Talk all you want about the Bible, the
What, When, Where -- Why and How
And talk about God's love for all the world
Then and only then is your talk "news-worthy"
04.09.83

VICTORY PROCLAIMED

A Christmas wreath
Pinned to your lapel
Shouts out the cry of victory
By our Lord's defeat of hell

A Christmas chaplet
Worn with dignity and pride
Marks our Savior's honor
Before all nations far and wide

A Christmas garland
By the promise of God's Word
Proclaims our death to sin and the
Resurrection of Christ our Lord
12.25.83

PEACE OF MIND
SHALOM

Peace of mind is found
  In repose upon Christ's breast
He is the only refuge
  Where we can find sweet rest

Our emptiness is filled
  And He satisfies our thirst
He is the living fountain
  Each time we put Him first

All anger is replaced
  By the kindness of His love
Our broken hearts are mended
  By His Spirit from above

He fully paid the price
  When He died upon this earth
He is truly God in man
  Through the uniqueness of His birth

Let not your heart be troubled
  For His Holy Spirit reigns near
Just put your trust in Jesus
  All petitions He will hear

If you're too busy doing "good works"
  You may fail to hear His "call"
Keep your eyes always on Jesus
  And give to Him your all
02.28.83

THE MYSTERY OF HOPE

When you can't escape the events of life
   The way you handle the pain and strife
      That's the *Mystery* of Hope

Hope is not a tangible thing
   But it's a reality that makes our hearts sing
      That's the *Secret* of Hope

Hope's the blessing God gives as a tool
   To help us overcome the bitter and cruel
      That's the *Gift* of Hope

When the problems of life are too hard to bear
   Change your direction and know God is there
      That's the *Power* of Hope

God has promised He will be there
   No matter what troubles you have to bear
      That's the *Guarantee* of Hope

When you believe God knows what is best
   And you trust Him for all the rest
      That's the *Acceptance* of Hope
03.18.06

BEYOND FORGIVENESS

You cannot be a victim of your past
Except by your own consent
For God's grace is greater by far
Than all the worst that's ever been

He patiently waits for you to choose
The forgiveness He has given
By using the worst to bring forth good
He even goes beyond forgiveness

You will no longer be a victim of your past
If only you will allow God to give to you
That which goes beyond forgiveness --
God's unconditional, unmerited love
02.02.02

1 TIMOTHY 2:3-6

"...This is good and acceptable in the sight of God our Savior, who desires all men to be saved and to come to the knowledge of the truth. For there is one God, and one mediator between God and men, the man Christ Jesus, who gave Himself as a ransom for all..."

I WISH YOU JESUS

When you feel lonely
I wish you **Love**
When you feel sad
I wish you **Joy**
When you feel discouraged
I wish you **Hope**
When you feel anxious
I wish you **Peace**
When you feel lost
I wish you **Jesus**
04.10.09

JOHN 3:16

"...For God so loved the world that
He gave His only begotten Son
that whosoever believes in Him
should not perish
but have everlasting life..."

GOD'S MAYPOLE

Catch the streamers of God's Maypole
Seek His **Mercy** first of all
It is yours just for the taking
God is faithful to us all

Catch the streamers of God's Maypole
Hold his **Goodness** in your hand
Take the ribbon of His **Kindness**
Let Him wrap you with each strand

Catch the streamers of God's Maypole
Seize His **Love** and hold on tight
Partake in all He has to offer
Dance with Him with great delight

Catch each streamer of God's Maypole
Capture every strand of **Joy**
Celebrate His Holy Presence
His festivities employ

Catch the streamers of God's Maypole
Mercy, Goodness, Kindness--Love and Joy!
God gave them all to you, my friend
His blessings forevermore enjoy
04.11.83

MY ALPHA AND OMEGA

You are my Alpha and my Omega
You are my First and my Last
There is none other beside you
Whose love for me will last

No matter what I do or say
No matter where I go
You are always there beside me
My every step you truly know

You are my best friend
You are the One who died for me
Father God sent you as ransom
That I might live eternally

Thank you for your sacrifice
Thank you for your love
I truly want to serve you, Lord
And give you all my love
07.07.10

CRYSTAL INSPIRATIONS

"Echoes of Love"

LOVE IS IN THE AIR

Love is in the air
Let every Sweetheart girl and boy
Make a warm place in their hearts
Then snuggle together and enjoy

Love is in the air
Affectionately sitting by the fire
Sweethearts warm and cuddly
Are filled with amorous desire
02.14.89

THE ESSENCE OF LOVE

Love starts softly and slowly
Develops beautifully, gradually
All things love can weather

A tender touch says it all
Reflecting a replica of your love
Bringing us closer together

We search diligently to find
The essence of life's intrinsic nature
Love's essential being -- is our answer
07.15.71

WHAT IS *LOVE?*

What is love?
Defining love would be
To limit it for me

Love is like a mirror
By loving one another
We reflect each other

What is love?
Love is infinity
Sprinkled with serenity
04.20.71

WITHOUT **LOVE**

The years passed rapidly
Leaving unused love within my heart
There was an emptiness to be filled
Without love
Life is a waste
09.18.70

Notation: Before Emery, my heart had much unused love to give, After Emery came into my life, my heart now is full and overflows with love and significance.

LOVE'S REFLECTION

> " ...Be like a mirror which always
> takes the color of the thing it reflects,
> and which is filled by as many images
> as there are things placed before it"
> Leonardo De Vinci

Our love shines by reflection now
   With a luster soft and glistening
In the quietness of the night
   To love sounds I am listening

Our love has been intensified
   Although without design
Once we directed energies
   Toward actions oft unkind

Beyond the sphere of perception
   A mystical event began
Warm attachment, then deep affection
   Grew from what we found within

Continued

Destiny affected and accomplished
   More than we intended
It overcame our greatest faults
   And our marriage mended

We have completed the circle now
   From a journey out of sadness
Into a deep, compassionate love
   That fills my heart with gladness

Now loving you is delightful
   And again my heart is set afire
You have filled my life completely
   With amorous, intense desire

Love is passionate and unrelenting
   Surpassing all that has past
Substantiating the old adage --
   If it's **_true love_** -- it **will last**
05.23.78

LOVE-BUG SYNDROME

I will not write poems
 With words that aren't true
But I tend to get "mushy"
 When I write poems about **you**

I address you as "honey"
 Or my "sweet turtle-dove"
Poems seem to do this
 To people in love

I rip and I rave about
 What a great guy you are
I regress to a school girl
 Who is struck by a "star"

I hug and I kiss you
 And caress you again
Oh don't be so smug
 It's just with my pen

I'd smuggle you into
 My workplace each day
If by this brash act I could
 Be near you some way

I'm really relentless
 With the passion I feel
Intense with emotion
 Enthusiasm and zeal

You might comprehend
 That I've been afflicted
By the "love-bug syndrome"
 And it's to you I'm addicted
05.23.88

LOVE'S ENERGY

Beyond all time and space
In this or in another place
You're in my mind and heart
Love's made my living start

Wherever else you may go
Surely this you must know
My spirit with yours entwines
That is what love defines

Charisma can penetrate
What man can't contemplate
Your mark is on this world
Love's energy surrounds this girl
Yo te Amo
08.26.79

KISS ME ONCE

Kiss me once
Kiss me twice
Kiss me once again
Ooooh, that was soooo nice
Now Be My Valentine
My friend

KISS KISS KISS KISS KISSie you
02.14.08

101

THAT'S PART OF LOVING

Lying quietly beside you
  With your body touching mine
Dropping off to dreamland
  With thoughts of you in mind
    --that's part of loving

Waking early in the morn
  With you is such a pleasure
You're so happy and content
  A blessing without measure
    --that's part of loving

With appetites so similar
  Cooking is an easy chore
But eating meals together
  Is the part that I adore
    --that's part of loving

Waiting to hear your footsteps
  Knowing you'll soon be here
Is one of my daily joys
  I look forward to, my dear
    --that's part of loving

Continue

I love our long vacations
  All the places we have been
We travel well together
  You're my lover and my friend
    --that's part of loving

When we work together
  Our energies we combine
It's great to have a partner
  Who inspires you all the time
    --that's part of loving

There're times we just talk quietly
  Yet we've had a fight or two
Making-up is so delightful
  Even fighting's fun with you
    --that's part of loving

Work or play or quiet times
  I like to spend with you
We 're so synchronized
  It's a pleasure loving you
    --that's the best part of loving
07.26.83

Dedicated to my husband, lover, partner, friend and inspiration,
Emery Tuttle; he is the best part of loving...

CHANGES

Moments go
Life changes
Nothing stays the same

Sometimes you must
Give up good things
For better things

But nevertheless
It's always hard
To change
07.04.77

I'M SENDING YOU MY SMILE

I'm sending you my smile
Please put it on and wear it
It will perk you up when
You think you can not bear it

Remember even a little smile
Will cause your face to wrinkle
But it's **really** not an ugly wrinkle
It's only a cute little twinkle
04.30.09

104

AWARENESS

I want to share with you
The innermost things
Even the impossible

I wish I had known you
In all the years gone by
Sharing all of life together

I want to be aware of you
Interested in your being
Hearing what you say

I also want you to penetrate me
To experience my inner being
And understand my intrinsic nature

I want the future with you to be
Me aware of you and
You aware of me
09.29.77

LOVE SONGS IN THE NIGHT

Music quietly playing
Mellow-sweet sounds ringing
Bringing lingering ecstasy
And melancholic dreaming

Warmth thoughts come to heart
Memories of days gone by
The glow of excitement kindled
Sparkling teardrops fill my eyes

Tender, romantic sounds
Familiar old love-songs
Mysteriously enticing
In a way all their own

Never hesitating
The melody rings on
Cheerfully announcing
Love's tenderness in song

Listening wistfully to
A sentimental love-song
Dreaming of days gone by
Playing love-songs all night long
12.01.75

YO TE AMO
I LOVE YOU

I just want to say "I love you"
Just because you're you

Your tender heart and kindness
Is genuine through and through
02.14.07

CRYSTAL INSPIRATIONS

"Tiny Glimpses of
My Family"

CRYSTAL INSPIRATIONS

"Tiny Glimpses of My Family"

My Husband

JoANNE Tuttle
08.29.10

Happy 90th Birthday, Emery W. Tuttle

Emery W. Tuttle was born August 29, 1920, in Johnson Creek, Wisconsin. He moved to Texas in 1945 after WW II, where he had served as a 2nd Lieutenant. in the 820th Bomb Squadron of the 7th Army Air Force. He had 51 bombing missions in the Central Pacific where he earned the Metal of Honor. He married and had four children.

We were married in 1971. We now live at Cedar Creek Lake, near Gun Barrel City, Texas, which is seventy-five miles southeast of Dallas.

Many of my poems are dedicated to him because he is my soul-mate, lover, friend.

GRANDFATHER......HIM?

If you like to hear stories
Of the days long gone by
Come sit by your grandfather
And stories will fly

He'll carry you back
To his own boyhood days
With adventurous stories
Of his mischievous ways

He'll even tell you
About history and such
And all of the things
That he loves so much

Come sit beside him
Give him a hug and a smile
He'll tell you great stories
To entertain you a while

If you should get wiggly
And fidgety, too
Reach up and give him
A big kiss or two

You mustn't forget
That a hug and a kiss
Are the only two things
He can never resist!
04.10.79

Dedicated to him...your grandfather, great-grandfather, great-
great grandfather, Emery Tuttle, a remarkable man.

EMERY'S SPACE

Today I came into your space
We walked that space as one
Singing, dancing, laughing, talking
It was such a day of fun

I thought you might be troubled
To share your space with me
But you just sang a love-song
Then gave **all** your space to me

Today was just the first day
Of the same space we must share
Certainly **I** would not want space
Where **you** could not be there

Since you gave all your space to me
I will give you all of mine
We'll walk that space together
Hand-in-hand 'til the end of time
09.01.94

Dedicated to the first day of my retirement and to my loving husband Emery. For the previous twenty years before my retirement, Emery worked out of our home. Now that I was retiring, we would be sharing the space at home together all day. To my surprise, it was great to share space with him even though I like noise and activity and he likes peace and quiet.

114

EMERY'S GETTING BOLDER

We have celebrated your birthday
Anytime or place we took a notion
We whooped it up high up in the air
Even celebrated it on the ocean

I guess I have forgotten
The actual day, my dear
So I'll send you birthday greetings
Every day throughout the year

Year 2000 is a good time
To be getting a little older
In the year "ought-ought" nothing
Should keep you from acting bolder

When your birthday comes in 2001
It will be easier to get through
Because then the century will be
Getting older...right along with you!
08.29.00

Dedicated to a happy 80th birthday to my dear husband, Emery,
August 29, 2000 (the year ought-ought).

ON EMERY'S 80TH BIRTHDAY

Love to You

Watching all the love for you
From your friends that flow
I realize you truly are
Someone nice to know

I wish for you great peace
Throughout the coming year
May all your dreams come true
That you especially hold dear

May the Lord richly bless you, and
Keep you in all your ways
Bringing you joy and happiness
In all the coming days
08.29.00

FRESH START

Take courage
Don't fret
Put old mistakes away
Start life anew today

Be not burdened
Be not anxious
Forgiven is your sin
So make a fresh start again

Take joy
Be glad
God watches over you
His Word is always true
01.01.84

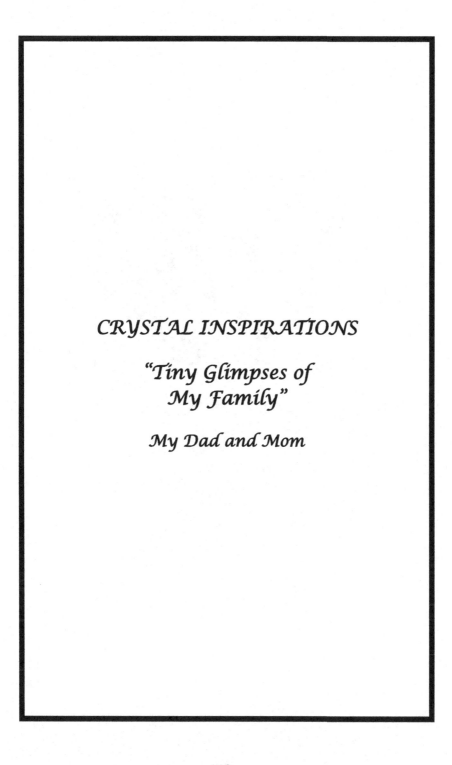

CRYSTAL INSPIRATIONS

"Tiny Glimpses of
My Family"

My Dad and Mom

JACK EDGAR THOMPSON, Sr   AGNES ELIZABETH STONE
(1910-1976)   THOMPSON
                            (1914-1981)

MY DAD AND MOM

TEXAS STYLE FATHER'S DAY

...This Father's Day
We wish you a Texas style
Giddy up, Giddy up go!!
Go Dad Go!!
Happy Father's Day
06.19.08

Dedicated to all fathers and to those who have lost their father.
I miss my dad and think of him often.

MOTHERS ARE SPECIAL

Wishes are written just once a year
To send you greetings and bring you cheer
Let these wishes be felt all year round
Even though they weren't written down

Every mother wants to know
That all her children love her, so
Although we don't always say the word
I hope, dear mom, our love is heard

We wish you a
Happy Mother's Day with love
05.01.12

Dedicated to all mothers and to those who have lost their mother.
I miss my mom and think of her often, especially on Mothers' Day.

MY DAD

My Dad was just a "*tiny*" man
Five feet five in stocking feet
That was as tall as he could stand
But a man like him you cannot beat

My Dad was not a "*little*" man
In my eyes he always stood
Like a "*giant*" ten feet tall
The way every daddy should

My Dad was not a "*weak*" man
He had the strength of ten his size
He could do the hardest tasks
That you could visualize

My Dad was a "*fix-it*" man
Without complaint he would begin
To fix anything that was broken
And make it work again

My Dad was a "*Jack-of-all-trades*" man
There was nothing he couldn't do
"*Jack*" was the perfect name for him
He could fix anything for you

My Dad was a "*hard-working*" man
Providing for his kids and wife
He never shirked a single task
He worked hard all his life

My Dad, *per* mom, was an "*important*" man
There was nothing for her he wouldn't do
He loved her with all his heart
For forty-six years their love was true
Continued

My Dad was a "*tender*" man
He listened to my tales of woe
He helped me with my problems
And never said, "*I told you so*"

My Dad was a "*loving*" man
Every baby caught his eye
He loved dogs, cats and kids
And the elderly, he'd not pass by

My Dad was a "*proud*" man
He took pride in all he did
But he was proudest of his family
From the oldest to the last grandkid

My Dad was a "*generous*" man
With money, gifts and time
He depended upon mom to buy the gifts
Although I'm sure she didn't mind

My Dad was **not** a "*patient*" man
When things didn't exactly go his way
He could yell and scream and throw a fit
And say the things only sailors say

My Dad was a "*steadfast*" man
Always there if we're sick or money was short
He was always there to rescue me when
The washer broke or the car wouldn't start

My Dad was an "*in-law*" man
A devoted son-in-law they would agree
A kind and loving brother-in-law was he
And a generous father-in-law, you see
Continued

My Dad was a "*loving*" man
My maternal grandmother never knew
He wasn't really **her** son, because he
Treated her like a natural son should do

My Dad was a "*family*" man
A pillar on which we could all depend
He would never let us down
He loved us to the end

My Dad means more to me than
Any poem can show how I feel
Or how much I've missed him
And how I miss him still

Two questions I wish I'd asked *my Dad*
One was, "What's your **best memory** of me?"
And the other, "What **memory of you**
Would you leave for my never-ending legacy?"

It is *fitting* these questions were never asked
Probably he could not have answered them
Because I know he liked **all of me**
And I want **all of my memories** of him
06.18.78 (Father's Day 1978, missing you)

Dedicated to the loving memory of my dad, Jack Edgar
Thompson, Sr. (1910-1976). He died much too soon. I love him
still and miss him so. I am reminded of all the countless, unselfish
things he did for me and my little family.

ECHOES OF VALENTINES PAST

Although his lips are now silent
There echoes in her mind
All the times that he told her
She was his valentine

Those words have much meaning
Out of love they were spoken
His love still lingers with her
She needs no other token

As the years slipped by quietly
She knew his love was there
Always she'll be his sweetheart
An eternal bond they share

No longer can she hear his words
Only memories are left, you see
She knows they still are sweethearts
And cherishes his love and memory
02.14.78

REAL LOVE

Real love is only given

By a person free to choose
And love that's freely given
Is a love you'll never lose
02.14.77

Dedicated to my mom, Agnes Elizabeth Stone Thompson,(1914-1981), a valentine thought for her in lieu of those valentines fate took away when my dad, Jack E. Thompson, Sr., died in 1976. Happy Valentine's Day, mom, this time it's from me.

Yo Te Amo

I know my daddy loved you
    With all his soul and heart
He always thought about you
    As every day would start

No matter how he wrote it
    The meaning was the same
He wanted to say, "I love you"
    And below it sign his name

He tried to make things easy
    For you to do your work
There really wasn't any task
    That he would ever shirk

He nailed it up -- or tore it down
    Whatever you wanted done
He'd put an outlet on **every** wall
    If you just wanted one

Whenever holidays rolled around
    He'd buy a gift or two
The only thing that was in his heart
    Was to give the best to you

Continued

126

I know my daddy loved you
  With all his soul and heart
And it was never in his plan
  For you to have to part

Just keep his memories with you
  Then his love won't fade away
You'll meet again in Heaven
  And love again some day

Don't let this poem distress you
  For life cannot be changed
You must continue on without him
  And your lifestyle rearrange

Know that he wished for you the best
  It's hard to understand
But if it were within his power
  He'd be with you 'til the end

I know my daddy loved you
  And you really loved him, too
Yo te amo to my dad – and to mom
  Because I love both of you
05.19.78

Dedicated to my dad (1910-1976) and to my mom (1914-1981).
Written for and dedicated to my mom after the death of my dad.
Now both have gone on to be with God and I miss them both.
    -- Yo te Amo to my dad and mom.

HEARTACHE

I know your heart is heavy
And your burdens hard to bear
I want to bring you comfort
And let you know I care

I'm sure you must feel helpless
All alone just waiting there
Wondering if God will choose
Again his life to spare

There are no words to soothe you
In your distress and heart-felt sorrow
Yet you're not bereft of hope
You can trust God for tomorrow

When you're undergoing grief
You must try to do your best
To reach out in expectation
And bear-up under stress

I know how much you love him
It's reflected in your face
And I know if it were possible
You would even take his place

Continued

But you're not allowed to suffer
For another whom you love
There's a purpose for all that happens
Known only to God above

A mother's love cannot be measured
No boundaries does love make
She loves each of her children
And would suffer for their sake

I'm glad you have a tender heart
And are such a loving mother
I would not exchange you even
If I could choose to another

In this your time of heartache
Please know that I do care
And anytime you need me
I will always be right there
10.11.78

Dedicated to my mother as she waits for word of her son's,(my brother), pending brain tumor surgery. God is a merciful God and will never allow more than we can bear and He will walk all paths with us always; hence, we are comforted.

THE CONQUERING FORCE

Warming, fiery rays of God's love
Strip our burdens all away
Casting them into endless time
Bringing welcomed peace our way

Love's the only conquering force
That sweeps away the burning past
Accept it gladly, be not afraid
God's precious love forever lasts

Limit not what God can do
Uproot that channel blocker -- *sin*
When God unfolds His perfect way
Let His quiet, flowing peace come in

Reflect on God's enormous power
Harmful thoughts must be turned out
Grasp His everlasting truth
Remove that destructive force of doubt

Look upon us with your favor, Lord
All our efforts avail us naught
Dwell in us; unfold your truth, Lord
For by Thy Spirit we are taught

We treasure every hour with you, Lord
Rejoicing in you day by day
Abiding in your perfect love
Your conquering force, which is our stay
10.17.83

Notation: Written on the anniversary of the death of my mother, Agnes Elizabeth Stone Thompson (1914-1981). God conquers grief. My mother was killed in 1981 in a auto accident. My father died in 1976 with cancer. My brother died in 1979 after a long bout with brain cancer. By 1983, God's comfort was my only stay.

PRAYING FOR HIS RECOVERY

God grant him peace and comfort
And may these gifts remain
To keep him cheered and
strengthened
Until he is well again
We are praying daily that a full
Recovery he'll soon regain
10.15.04

CRYSTAL INSPIRATIONS

"Tiny Glimpses of My Family"

My Grandmother

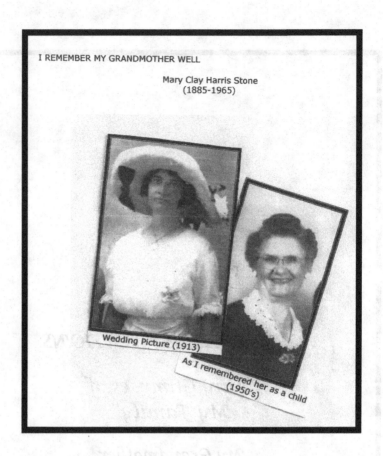

I REMEMBER MY GRANDMOTHER WELL

Mary Clay Harris Stone
(1885-1965)

Wedding Picture (1913)

As I remembered her as a child
(1950's)

Mary Clay Harris Stone was born in 1885. She was married to John E. Stone for over fifty years. They had one daughter, my mother, Agnes Elizabeth Stone Thompson.

My grandmother was the best Christian example I have ever known. She was the most loving and giving person ever. You didn't come to her home without leaving with something: a bouquet of flowers from her yard; a bowl of fresh soup from her kitchen; or some little thing she made by hand. She never had many worldly goods but she was affluent in spiritual treasures.

I REMEMBER MY GRANDMOTHER WELL

I remember my grandmother well
The kindest person I've ever known
There was nothing she wouldn't do for me
Anytime I visited her home

My comfort she would worry about
Was I hungry, cold or sick?
If there was anything I wanted
She would hurry to fix it quick

She never had much money
Yet she always had something to give
All she had she shared with others
Although meagerly she lived

Her heart was made of purest gold
She never said a word unkind
She was the finest woman on this earth
None like her could I ever find

I remember the many times
She comforted all my distress
She would always kiss away my hurts
With her love and tenderness

I think of her so often
Her love I'll never forget
I remember things she taught me
As thought she were with me yet

You won't read about her
In any history book
But I want to be just like her
And follow the path she took
Continued

She would let us do some things
At home we couldn't do
We'd make mud pies in her kitchen
But our mother never knew

Whenever I was sick
She would always bring me
A big bowl of chicken soup
Because it made me well, you see

She had her little garden
The soil she'd gently till
Squash and ripe tomatoes
I remember these things still

She'd go from dawn to dusk
As busy as a bee
She grew such pretty flowers
And gave bouquets to me

What she had, she gave away
Nothing for herself she kept
For all the love she gave to me
Many tears for her I've wept

She made each of us a little quilt
Not like any we could buy
With bits of cloth and tiny stitches
Something to remember her by

I still have that little quilt
And other trinkets here and there
But I don't really need these things
To remember her love and care
05.21.78

She had the deepest love for me. From within her heart it came.
No matter what I was or did she'd love me just the same. I miss
her immeasurably.

Kiss Pills

I'm sending you a get well remedy
That my grandmother gave to me
Whenever I would get an "awie"
This is what she did for me

It always seemed to work, you see
It never seemed to fail to be
The very, very best remedy
That anyone ever gave to me

In her arms she would hold me
Warm and cozy it would be
Then she would start to kiss me
On all the places hurting me

One by one with my pain relieved
Much better I always seemed to be
If I needed one more kiss then she'd
Give one more little kiss to me

I'm sending you her kissing-remedy
A bottle of kiss pills for you from me
Take one as needed and you will see
A kiss or two is the very best remedy
04.26.10

Kiss Kiss Kiss Kiss Kiss Kiss Kiss Kiss Kiss Kiss

Dedicated to my grandmother, Mary Clay Harris Stone, (1885-1965) She always had tender, loving care for me. She kissed my tears away. I loved her dearly and have missed her immensely.

WRINKLES ARE BEAUTIFUL

I want to grow old gracefully
As my Grandmother seemed to do
She didn't mind the wrinkles
That came as old she grew

She would just keep on smiling
A frown she could not abide
She said frowns make the wrinkles
That she would want to hide

But wrinkles made by smiles, she'd say
Make your face just shine and glow
Then you will be much happier
As those wrinkles start to show

And you will hardly notice
The grooves that time has made
Although you'll still grow older
But your true beauty will not fade
05.21.85

Dedicated (on her birth date May 21st) to the memory of my grandmother, Mary Clay Harris Stone, (1885-1965).She had true beauty until the very end. I miss her even now. Her wrinkles were all smile creases and were so beautiful.

PROVERBS 31:30

*"...Charm is deceitful and
beauty is vain, But a
woman who fears the Lord
she shall be praised..."*

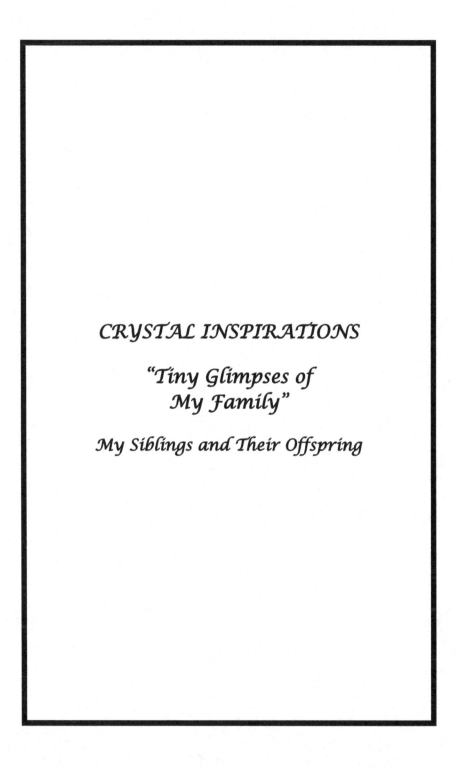

CRYSTAL INSPIRATIONS

"Tiny Glimpses of My Family"

My Siblings and Their Offspring

Jack Edgar Thompson, Jr.
(09.05.36 — 01.12.79)
MY "BUDDY"

ETERNAL BOND

I love you
The words echo softly now because
In the days gone past I haven't said them often
So now I dare not shout them out lest
You think them weak and insincere

Nonetheless I've love you
Through these many years
Whether or not I've seen you often
Is not the determinant of love's depth nor the
Quality of love -- love spans time and distance

Love continues throughout our lives
I have but few childhood memories of you
Because I left home much too soon
I know little of your lifestyle even now
Yet my heart is entwined in yours

Love endures all things
For these many years
Only the seasons of joy brought us together
Yet at no time did the long separations
Spoil our closeness or steal our love away

Love is eternal
Without contact, still we knew each other well
We do not know the details of our beings
However nothing is taken from us
We have always belonged together
Continued

Love does not ever change in depth or quality
And I would not change our lifestyles
Or even wish for a closer relationship with you
For had we known each other better
Perhaps we would have grown apart and distant

You are and always have been so loving
I know you are good, affectionate and kind
You have conveyed these passions to me
There's no condemnation for infrequent contact
Perhaps a little disappointment or wishful longing

I declare my love for you
May that phenomenon between us
That for so long has held our bond intact, now be
Strengthened even more in this your hour of need
I would if I could give strength from my own soul

I love you with deep abiding love
My life is richer because of you
In every way I'm glad you touched my life
My life is blessed by yours
For you are my brother
08.12.78

Dedicated to my brother, Jack Edgar Thompson, Jr., suffering
from brain tumors, so young a man, so dear a brother. Although
we have spent many years apart, our love endured time.

CONSOLE MY HEART,

Don't you hear my anguish?
Can't you feel my grief?
Won't you please just hold me
Until I can find relief?

I want you just to touch me
To hold me in your arms
To feel my aching heart
To keep me from all harm

I try to comprehend this
Please help me see somehow
I need to find some peace
And really don't know how

Hear my aching heart
Don't throw me just a "straw"
By saying that "I need not cry"
That won't comfort me at all

Life looks to me so gloomy now
Existence bleak and sad
I'm unable to find real value
Nor some hope to make me glad

When I get weak and weary
I really need a friend
Just let me know you love me
Please touch me once again
12.23.78

Notation: During this sad time in my life, waiting for news of the outcome of my brother's surgery for a terminal illness, holidays are not the same this year. I need my family and friends for consolation, compassion and strength. God gives us each other for a helping hand during times of sorrow.

HOW HEAVY ART THOU, MY HEART

How heavy art thou, my heart; intense with pain
I feel as though I shall never lift this burden
Remembering my neglect in days gone by adds
An unmerciful heaviness to my grieving heart

Visions of a future forever separating us and
Depriving me from ever touching your life again
Indeed intensely increases that pain I feel
And my heart unceasingly aches in grief

Holidays once were a season of joy for us
Now only bring me dismay and agony
Yet I know I must eradicate this hopelessness
And fill my heart with courage and expectancy

A hapless event has stricken without warning
Although it was not altogether unrelenting
For we were granted a small benevolence of time
To express the unspoken; to right any reproach
11.23.78

Notation: A token of time was granted us in the days of the grave
illness of my brother, Jack E. Thompson, Jr. He lies at death's
door suffering with brain tumors. Although we were never close in
days past, God granted grace for us to have reconciliation of our
bond of love...time to say "good-bye."

SORROW FILLS MY DAY

In the hour of my distress, I sought empathy
Avowing only feeling loved would satisfy my grief
This yearning for comfort I hoped to find in you

I am dismayed by the crumbling straws
Lying scattered in my mind; so
I barred my mind against the emptiness

Comfort was not mine to have
To fortify myself against life's storm
There were only broken pieces

My soul lay barren and forlorn
I was perplexed by hurt and pain
Buried deep within my soul

But no comfort or solace awaited me
From within the realm of my mortal self
For unheard went my appeal

A bitter cold surrounded me
The barrier I could not break
Nothing could penetrate the icy walls
Continued

Nor bestow warmth for me again
While the agony of grief upon me befell
Howbeit there is nothing to call upon

Nor anyone to share my sorrow with
Nor substitute for what in me should be
Have I made comfort so idealized

The requirements are so demanding
They never can be realized
Charging it to be all encompassing

Forbidding it to fail me
True I have epitomized being love
Yet love cannot be my equipoise

Oh such sorrow in my heart and soul
There's no escaping your wretchedness
I alone with you must deal

Alas my days are filled with deep sorrow
No one can experience agony *for* me
Nor alleviate this pain I feel
11.22.78

UNDERSTANDING DEATH

Why should this be
This unfamiliar entity?
Where is the peace
In this inevitable certainty?

Death brings such grief
There's no infinitesimal relief
It is part of life's cycle
But life is so very brief

Unavoidable is this fate
It's as close as one breath
It is common to all
No favorites has *Death*

When this voyage occurs
A change we must make
But a significant loss
Will be left in the wake

When *Death* has come near
A numbness you feel
In anger you shout
Then bargain a *deal*
Continued

I'm not ready just yet
This intruder to greet
Preparations are needed
Before we can meet

Grant me one moment
To arrange things around
For this treacherous journey
Where no repeal's found

When it comes to the end
Death's the one who will win
With quiet resignation
I must make *Death* my friend

From the dawn of mankind
There's one mystery we find
When *Death* comes to you
Your *death's* also mine

In all things they say
A purpose must play
But I don't understand
Why you *died* today
01.12.79

Notation: The day my brother, Jack Edgar Thompson, Jr.,
"Buddy" (1936-1979) died.

MEMORIES

Your gentleness touched the earth
   N'er a summer breeze
Could so gentle be, nor
   So inclined to please

A softness whispered by
   Lightly touching all in reach
Each and every passerby
   Changing the life of each

Whence came this gentleness
   Could it not linger more
There are many wonders
   Left waiting to explore

'Twas for a few short moments
   Like the short-lived, driven snow
You tenderly touched the earth
   Then suddenly you go

You barely touched my life
   But your imprint upon my heart
Will forever linger there
   Your memory to impart
01.12.80

Dedicated to the memory of my brother, Jack E. Thompson, Jr. (1936-1979); who touched my life with love and tenderness and passed from this earth too soon.

GRIEF

Every person's death diminishes us a little
We grieve
Not as much for the deceased
As it is for our self -- our loss
Grief is the healing process
God's healing balm
That overcomes that loss
We miss what that person contributed
to our life, so
We grieve -- our loss
02.18.08

AN AURA OF NOBILITY

Born with a natural curiosity
Exploring all the world around
Discovering first his little fingers
Then his toes he found

With crystal-clear blue eyes
And that impish little smile
He could dazzle the embassy ball
Although he's just a child

He presents a tender portrait
Of a young aristocrat
Irresistibly dashing
Charming and all of that

He acts pleasantly blasé
Until things don't go his way
Then like lightning's electric voice
There's a turbulent display

With his aristocratic spirit
A leader he will be
For he has that splash of confidence
And an aura of nobility
01.13.09

Dedicated to my great-great nephew, Cason Brock Eakin (01.13.09).
(He is the grandson of my niece, Glenda Thompson Eakin; who is the
daughter of my brother, "Buddy," Jack E. Thompson, Jr., (1936-
1979).I am so sorry my brother will not see his little grandson grow
up because he loved children so very much and would have
thoroughly enjoyed this aristocratic little boy.

A LIFETIME
Forging Ahead

Chubby, pink cheeks
Sparkling, blue eyes
Hair as golden as day

Tiny, tiny fingers
Busy as bees
Nimble with frolic and play

Cuddling, snuggling
In his mother's arms
This wee, wee baby lay

Growing tall, growing strong
With a lifetime forging ahead
To accomplish whatever he may
05.02.09

Dedicated to my great-great nephew, Tristan Riley Tucker (09.23.09). (He is the second grandson of my niece, Glenda Thompson Eakin .who is the daughter of my brother, "Buddy," Jack E, Thompson, Jr., (1936-1979).

Sonja Joyce Thompson Trott (10.23.38), my only sister. She married Wayne Trott and has four children, Gary, Patsy, Jacque and John. Wayne died in 1989.

Joyce lives about fifty miles from me in Brownsboro, Texas. She is not only my younger sister, but she is also "shorter." We used to call her "Little Bit."

SONJA JOYCE THOMPSON TROTT...
Numero Uno Sister

I have a younger sister
As red-headed as she can be
But every time I need her
She's always there for me

She lives quite some distance
And our visits have been few
But that doesn't seem to hinder
Our love from being true

Our lives have been quite different
We have taken separate paths
When we compare our problems
It makes for lots of laughs

For in all the ways we're different
There's as many we're the same
I guess that's because a long time ago
We shared the same last name
Continued

156

She had **lots** of children
I had **only** three
Well **actually** she had four
But that seems a **lot** to me!

She can paint and sing and write
All her kids her steps ensue
Her husband not to be left out
Learned to play the banjo, too

Her life is such a whirlwind
With her kids and all they do
But if you have a problem
She'll take time out just for you

She's brilliantly creative
With deep commitment and affection
She's my numero uno sister
And wins hands-up in that election
07.31.78

Dedicated to Sonja Joyce Thompson Trott, numero uno sister.
We never see eye-to-eye on anything...but that's because she is
a lot shorter than I am Actually, she is my only sister. I just don't
know Spanish well enough to say she's my only sister in Spanish,
so, Numero Uno is the best I can do.

LOOKING MY BEST

Ring-a-ling, Ring-a-ling
Hello there, my dear
Would you like to go
With us girls here and there

Hello to you, my friend
Why, certainly I would
I've always tried to go
Every place I could

But there's just one thing
From you I must request
It certainly would help me
To look my very best

Please ask each of the girls
Their glasses not to bring
"The reason?" you are asking
Well now I will explain
Continued

Only one dress do I have
That I'm still able to wear
But it has just a little spot
And the tiniest, little tear

This one dress is so designed
To make my short leg look long
I know it's not the usual custom, and
This might be considered wrong

However if each one of you girls
Your glasses would not take
No one will even notice
This tiny, little mistake

Then I would feel much better
'Cause I'd know that they can't see
And they'd have to just imagine
How pretty I must be
04.10.81

Dedicated to my sister the seamstress/artist (code name: sjtt),
Sonja Joyce Thompson Trott, the short girl with one short leg (If
you will take notice, her name is shorter than mine, too! L0L) No
wonder we called her "Little Bit"

WAYNE BERNARD TROTT
(09.27.36—04.05.89)

Dedicated to my brother-in-law, Wayne Bernard Trott (1936-1989), the greatest banjo player west of the rest. A great loss to his family and friends.

WAYNE BERNARD TROTT...
THE LAST OF THE "BIG BANJOS"

I don't know what you do all day
I guess you sit and *think*
Or plan and make decisions
For those of lower rank

When you come home at night
As soon as you are able
The first stop that you make
Is to the kitchen table

You then may settle down awhile
To take a little nap
Until the kids disturb your sleep
With a rap-a-tap, tap, tap

Now that you're alert again, you'll
Find something to amuse you
You'll play a little banjo tune
To demonstrate what you can do

With kids going in every direction
I know that you stay busy
But keeping up at your age
Will put you in a tizzy

Well I hope not all is lost
To this fact I can attest
When everyone is finally gone
Then you can get some rest

So play your tune and sing awhile
Then finally go to bed
Tomorrow is another day
You must work to stay ahead
12.19.78

GARY WAYNE TROTT

Gary Wayne Trott, my sister's oldest son. He is still to this day a man of integrity and perseverance.

GARY WAYNE TROTT...
The Boy With A Tenacious Perseverance

Gary, the Minister of the Mop
Filled with inherent integrity
You attend to every duty
With a conscientious ability

Endowed with a tenacious perseverance
And a courageous appeal
You are invariable dependable
And filled with dauntless zeal

Because of your deep commitment
In high esteem you're held
Your duties you never shirk
Against authority you don't rebel

You have a splash of confidence
An inner resource to see you through
You are addicted to hard work
And faithful in all you do

May the values you now hold
Never diminish nor ever wane
As you fulfill your high aspirations
May you always stay the same
12.18.78

Dedicated to my nephew, Gary Wayne Trott, who tackles every task, even mopping the floor, with enthusiasm and integrity.

PATSY JOYCE TROTT THERIOT

Patsy Joyce Trott Theriot is my sister's oldest daughter. From the day she was born she was smiling at the world and everything in it. Her smiles are contageoous.

PATSY JOYCE TROTT...
The Girl With A Radiant Smile

---No one
Has ever smiled like you
   your dimples showing
   your face all glowing
You're radiant through and through

---Anything
Can make your smile come out
   your bright and sunny smiles
   sparkling for miles and miles
Sending happiness all about

---Always
Your smile brings joy into our hearts
   you penetrate the gloom
   throughout the entire room
As soon as that sunny smile starts

---Never
Allow your radiant smiles to stop
   you are contagious, you know
   when you let a smile show
We all want to catch what you've got
08.17.78

Dedicated to my niece, Patsy Joyce Trott Theriot, She has not
changed in all these years. Her smile still radiates the room.

Jacqueline Sue Trott Kendro is my sister's youngest daughter. This mischievous little girl could captivate you with her eyes. Time has not changed the penetrating, captivating power of her beautiful eyes.

JACQUELINE SUE TROTT...
The Girl With Penetrating Eyes

Full of immense pleasure
Her eyes become like exhilarating crescendos
Bursting with great happiness

Large, brown eyes, so refreshing, so infectious
Expressively beautiful
Reflecting a potpourri of emotions

So elegant for such a peerless creature
Her eyes pierce my heart
And captivate my very soul

Fascinating eyes, constantly changing
Rolling with incredulity or exasperation
Sparkling with mischief and frolic

Quietly she drops her eyelids in timidity
Fluttering them in a sultry, seductiveness
Yet she always remains warm and amiable

A quick and spontaneous animation
Activates the play of those eyes
To our delight and pleasure

Easy gusts of merriment
Bring a distinctive sparkle to her eyes
Yet these same eyes spit fire when angry

Beautiful eyes, capable of powerful sensitivity
Full of all human emotions
Continually penetrating our hearts
08.17.78

Dedicated to my niece, Jacqueline Sue Trott Kendro, who still
has beautiful, fascinating, penetrating eyes.

JOHN TROTT

John Bernard Trott is my sister's youngest son. He has always had a compassionate heart and a personal magic.

JOHN BERNARD TROTT...
The Boy With A Personal Magic

Sparkle, Sparkle, Sparkling...
Twinkling like a star
With a fiery spirit
Glowing near and far

With a personal magic...
Full of life and fun
With innocent mischievousness
You dazzle everyone

Full of perplexing questions...
Inquisitive and quick-witted
Mesmerizing us with impish charm
And the charisma you've emitted

Thoughtful and warmhearted...
As chivalrous as can be
With deep concern for people
You are love's epitome
12.18.78

Dedicated to my nephew, John Bernard Trott. A very adventurous
outdoorsy guy's guy full of warmhearted compassion, adventure
and love.

RICHARD LEE THOMPSON
(08.08.41–01.02.06)

MY BROTHER RICK

RICHARD LEE THOMPSON...
I wanted time to Know You better

I've attempted to reconstruct our lives
The picture was vague, the memories few
I left home much too soon and never
Got a chance to really know you

You were just a little boy
When I started married life
Soon after I became a mother
When I left home to be a wife

We didn't get an opportunity
To merge into each other's life
Your career was the Navy/work
Mine was being mother/wife

Growing into adulthood your life changed
You traveled the world; lived far away
Our different roads separated us
Preventing us together time day by day

The few times together brought us joy
We would love, laugh and play
You're still my little brother
And I love you very much today

Continued

172

Years have slipped by quickly
Neglect has brought regret
Although we've not been close
Nonetheless I love you yet

If we'd known what fate had in store
Probably we would have made more time
To know and appreciate each other more
Because I'm your family and you are mine

We let the years slip by quickly
As many people do
I thought I'd always have more time
To really get to know you

But sudden illness overtook you
Without much warning or reprieve
It did not give us much time
For our regrets to be relieved

I think about you often now
And all the time that we let go by
Lamenting our disregard and neglect
Until fate forced us to say good-bye
Continued

Providence provided us a moment
To bid each other our last adieu
Allowing me time to say to my brother
I have always genuinely loved you

I wanted another opportunity
To make amends for disregarded time
But that destiny was not possible
The prospect was not yours...or mine

I'll remember you always
And love you in my heart
I've learned the lesson of neglect
And the regret that it will impart

I've discovered to keep life current...now
Is the only way to live without regrets
And to never take life for granted...so
When life ends...there'll be no unpaid debts
01.02.06

Dedicated to my youngest brother, Richard Lee Thompson. (1941-2006). I must acknowledge my deep regret that I did not make the time or effort to get to know him better before he was stricken with cancer. By the time cancer strikes, it is too late to make amends for years of neglecting a relationship that is actually based on love, but disregarded because we mistakenly believe we have all the time in the world to relate to someone we love. I am grateful to God that he allowed me that last moment of reprieve to tell my brother that I loved him.

CRYSTAL INSPIRATIONS

"Tiny Glimpses of My Family"

My Three Sons

DONALD

LARRY

DAVID

MY THREE SONS

DONALD...
Just Remember This

After a while it appears to me
That having birthdays
Will stop making you smile
Because they come so fast

You used to celebrate birthdays
One by one, year by year...it's true
But now it seems that an entire
Decade passes by in-between

Then more decades pass by quickly
And before you know it
Birthdays advance rapidly to
30--40--50 years of time

Then you'll need to celebrate
Birthdays by the century
But this year it's not yet that late
You're still in your first century

Go ahead and really celebrate today
As you're headed toward that big 1-0-0...
After a while you'll begin to forget
How many birthdays have passed your way
04.25.09

Dedicated to my great grandfather #1 son, Donald Ray Holcomb,
(05.02.52) who is rapidly creeping up on 60 and a century of time.
He is trying to be as old as I am. LoL. Soon I'm going to forget
which one of us *is* the oldest.

LARRY...
My Joy

What a joy I would have missed
Had you not been born
All the love I ever had from you
From my heart would now be torn

So sympathetic and warm-hearted
You're my most compassionate son
You pour out to me such tenderness
As no one else has done

You're aware of all my feelings
Whatever my mood might be
If I'm sad you understand it
When I'm glad, you're glad with me

On that brisk November morn
When they announced another boy
I did not anticipate that
You would bring my life such joy

You have a dauntless spirit
So incredibly rare
Brimming with compassion
That marks how much you care
Continued

Your life's not stained by rivalry
Nor does hate in you abound
Instead you are most amiable
To everyone around

You're a conscientious, hard-worker
Yet so gentle and so kind
Such a sentimentalist
But oh, I'm so glad you're mine

The sheer pleasure of your good humor
Makes my heart leap out with joy
I'm a fortunate, wealthy woman
To have such a wonderful boy

As I watched you grow up
From a child into a man
I felt a twinge of pride
Someday you'll understand

My dreams for you from long ago
Are echoed in my pride
The love I have for you, my son
Will forevermore abide
11.07.78

Dedicated to my #2 son, Larry Bob Holcomb written on his 25th
birthday (11.07.53). This is 2012 and he is turning 59--more than
half a century old! The hills are singing happy birthday, Larry.

DAVID WAYNE...
My Little Cuddle Bug

Sweet as a summer rose
Sparkling as a star
Fierce as a lion you stand
A little cuddle bug you are

You melt me with your tiny arms
Winding 'round my neck so tightly
When you kiss me softly
And snuggle against me quietly

When you say, "I love you"
It thrills me through and through
So I want again to tell you
Just how much I love you, too
12.31.57

Dedicated to my last little cuddle-bug baby boy, my #3 son, David Wayne Holcomb, (01.08.55) My little red-headed cuddle-bug. He is now (in 2012) a grandfather himself. He has a daughter and son and four sweet little cuddle-bug grandbabies of his own. Time marches on.

CRYSTAL INSPIRATIONS

"Tiny Glimpses of My Family"

My Six Grandchildren

AMY HOLCOMB
FAIRCHILD

ALICIA HOLCOMB
TAYLOR

DAUGHTERS OF MY
SON, DONALD

TIFFANY HOLCOMB
TROWBRIDGE

MONIQUE HOLCOMB
STAPLETON

DAUGHTERS OF MY
SON , LARRY

SANDRA HOLCOMB
CHILD

CASEY WAYNE
HOLCOMB

CHILDREN OF MY
SON, DAVID

MY GRANDCHILDREN

All my little guys are parents now. Time flies by so fast unless you are sitting in a classroom waiting for the bell to ring.

AMY LaNETTE...
A Bright Ray of Sunshine

Amy LaNette with such big, pretty eyes
And a smile that charms me so
You're a bright ray of sunshine
And such a delight to know

Once you caused me anguish
When you came into this world
You turned me into a "grandmother"
Of my first bouncing baby grand-girl

My anxiety now has past
Because I have settled down
Now I'm called "grandmother"
By everyone around

You show so much excitement
In everything you do
Your eyes always sparkle
Like tiny drops of dew
Continued

You're lively -- full of questions
Wrinkling your perky little nose
And nothing boosts your enthusiasm
Like buying brand new clothes

You always entertain me
With stories of school and friends
You run and play all day
Your energy never ends

You're full of love and kindness
You're courteous and polite
I'm very proud of you
You are my heart's delight

Every time I see you
I know it's really true
The thrill within my heart
Is there because I really love you
07.04.79

Dedicated to my first grandchild, Amy LaNette Holcomb Fairchild,
(She is the oldest daughter of my oldest son, Donald). Amy now
(in 2012) has three children and three grandchildren of her own,
and I'm sure she understands the thrill to which I am referring.

AMY LaNETTE...
My Little Firecracker

My little firecracker granddaughter
Was born on the Fourth of July
She is always such a delight
And the apple of my eye

Her smile could always entice me
All her antics could make me smile
She was always full of mischief
But she was my pretty little doll

She's now a grown woman
With children of her own
And her own precious grandchildren
Have already come along

She grew up so fast
It put my head into a swirl
No matter how grown she is
She's still my little firecracker girl
07.04.10

Dedicated to my first granddaughter, Amy LaNette Holcomb Fairchild; happy 40th birthday. She was born on the Fourth of July. She is now a grandmother! My first grandchild/grandmother! That's special. Wow!

AMY LaNETTE...
--You Are Special--

It is said it takes only a minute
To find a special person
But you need to spend an hour
Before you can appreciate them

Then it would take at least a day
For you to learn to love them
After that you'd have a lifetime
Before you can forget them
04.17.09

Notation: I could not forget my little firecracker even in two
lifetimes because you are more than special, you were my first
adorable grandchild. All the other grandchildren are special also,
but you hold an unique place.

ALICIA ANN...
A Lingering Delight

With spontaneous gestures of affection
You keep me captivated
By a sweet and helpful disposition
You are motivated

You bewitch me with your smile
And the sparkle in your eyes
You are growing up so fast
And the time so quickly flies

You have very special qualities
Like no one else I know
A provocative independence
But that's why I love you so

I'm acutely aware of one thing
When you flash your sunny smile
I can't get mad at you
Even for a little while

With your charm and personality
You're a lingering delight
Sometimes you're full of questions
Other times you're very quiet
Continued

190

A tiny splash of freckles
Are etched across your nose
And some more missing teeth
Soon will be exposed

You are such a pleasure
And such a darling little girl
I love you more than anything
In this big, gigantic world
07.20.79

Dedicated to my granddaughter, Alicia Ann Holcomb Taylor (1973-2000). (Alicia is the youngest daughter of my son, Donald). I lost her due to cancer, a devastating loss. She left behind three beautiful children. She is missed.

IN TIME OF SORROW

Let the love of God
maintain your heart
during this time of
your deep sorrow
May you be strengthened
by the love of family and friends
and in the days ahead
may God bless you and keep you
and give you His perfect peace
comforting your heart with love
02.21.09

TIFFANY...
A Breath of Fresh Spring

Tiffany, Tiffany
Blue eyes and bright smile
Come sit beside me
Let's talk for a while

You're smart and you're bright
Just as cute as a bug
Come sit beside me
And give me a hug

Like a breath of fresh spring
With laughter and giggling
Not still for a moment
You're constantly wiggling

With delicate features
Framed by blond tresses
Penetrating blue eyes
And cute little dresses

Tiffany, Tiffany
Come sit for a while
Give me a hug
A kiss and a smile
03.27.79

Dedicated to my granddaughter, Tiffany Gaa Holcomb Wiggs Trowbridge, (Tiffany is my son Larry's oldest daughter). She now has three children of her own and some step-children who keep her busy, busy, busy. All that early childhood wiggling is paying off.

MONIQUE...
Life is Wonderful and Unique

Your life is just beginning
  Like mankind throughout the ages
Inviting diverse experiences
  To fill the empty pages

May you find a touch of beauty
  And learn truth held by the past
May you reflect upon life's treasures
  And value things that last

You'll always need a dream to dream
  And you'll need a goal to reach
There'll be lots of friends beside you
  Who'll be there to guide and teach

Life is full of wonders
  Imagination's always free
You have a lifetime of blank pages
  With splendid possibility

Yes life is filled with numerous joys
  For you, my little Monique
Your special dreams can come true
  For life is wonderful and unique
04.10.79

Dedicated to my newest granddaughter, Elizabeth Monique
Holcomb Stapleton. (Monique is my son Larry's second daughter
and my 10th grandchild). She is now (in 2012) the mother of two
unique little treasures of her own.

SANDRA...
My Sugar and Spice

With long blond tresses
   And sparkling blue eyes
This rosy-cheeked girl
   Is a delightful surprise

A warm-hearted creature
   This incredible child
Beguiles me continually
   With her irresistible smile

Her hugs and her kisses
   Are especially nice
She radiates love
   With sugar and spice

She's full of love and sweetness
   And kindness and more
There is not another child
   That I could love any more
01.07.79

Dedicated to my sweet granddaughter, Sandra Darlene Holcomb Child, (Sandra is the daughter of my youngest son, David). She radiates love, kindness and sweetness. She is now (in 2012) the mother of two little ones that are as sweet as she is and always has been. Sandra is made from "real" sugar (with a little spice).

194

CASEY WAYNE...
My Little Rug Rat

You're just a little rug-rat
A grubbing on the floor
A tiny little crumb-grabber
Always wanting something more

You cry and scream and throw a fit
When you don't get your way
But your mother thinks you're wonderful
And loves you more each day

Then your dad comes home at night
More attention you enjoy
It's evident to both of them
You're the "grandest" little boy

Your big sister thinks you're great
She will spoil you every day
She'll give you anything you want
And let you have your way

Grandfather Emery is the one
Who thinks you can do no wrong
Some day he'll write for you
A very special song

Only Grandmother Tuttle knows
Just exactly what you are
She isn't really **fooled** by you
She **knows...** you are the **best** by far
04.27.78

Dedicated to Casey Wayne Holcomb my only little grandson and
"My Little Rug-Rat" -- the best by far. (Casey is the son of my #3
son, David, and my only grandson.) He is now (in 2012) the
daddy of two little rug-rats of his own...my great grandchildren,
Grace and Andrew, who are totally adorable children.

CRYSTAL INSPIRATIONS

"Tiny Glimpses of My Family"

Some of My Great Grandchildren

CHELSEA
FAIRCHILD

JAMIE
HOLCOMB

KAYIEE
TAYLOR

MICHAEL
TAYLOR

ELIZABETH
CHILD

CHRISTOPHER
CHILD

GRACE
HOLCOMB

ANDREW
HOLCOMB

A FEW OF MY GREAT GRANDCHILDREN WITH POEMS FOLLOWING

CHELSEA...
You Have My Genes

You are the great granddaughter
Who must have all my genes
At least looking at all your antics
That is the way it seems

You are a happy, cheerful girl
And you are as smart as you can be
You are gracious and quite charming
That is just part of what I see

You bring life to all around you
And you have set your achievements high
You are looking for new adventures
With your cousin -- your ally

You challenge the waves in the ocean
And bury yourself in the sand
You jump high on the trampoline
Experiencing every new ordeal you can

One minute you are like a little monkey
With antics mischievously playful
Then next you look like a debutant
Bright eyed and amazingly beautiful
08.12.10

Dedicated to Chelsea LeeAnn Fairchild, my great granddaughter who acts the most like me. The exceptions are that she is much cuter, smarter and sweeter. She's such a delight to me and she has my genes.(Chelsea is the oldest child of my granddaughter, Amy, and the granddaughter of my oldest son, Donald).

JAMIE...
With A Dauntless Spirit

You have faced many painful obstacles
Life has not been a bed of roses
Your dauntless spirit of courage
Overcomes all that life imposes

I wish all those wounded moments
Could be magically repaired like new
Only God can intervene the past
And bring happiness and joy to you

You're headed for new adventures and
Crossing new and mysterious bridges
Be keenly aware God walks with you
Through the valleys, peaks, and ridges

Glorify God's name in every place
Continually praise Him in every way
God will be there to direct your path
And pour out rich blessings every day

There are no limits for your possibilities
The only obstacles in your way
Are not applying your imagination and
Not recognizing your potential every day
Continued

Savor every moment of your life
Because each moment is unique
Be vigilant in the decisions you make
Your future depends on what you seek

We have a common history
I desire to my share life with you
We'll have lots of laughs and a few tears
I'll pour forth God's blessings upon you
08.09.10

Dedicated to my great granddaughter Jamie Holcomb, (Jamie is the oldest daughter of my granddaughter, Alicia Holcomb Taylor (1973-2000)). I am so proud of Jamie's dauntless spirit and courage and look forward to seeing her potential grow.

JEREMIAH 29:11
"I know the plans I have for you,
Says the Lord...plans to prosper you, not
to harm you, plans to give you hope and
a future"

KAYLEE...
With the Cutest Dimples

I wrote about your mother
  Your aunt and cousins, too
But not until today had I
  Written about just *you*

You have the cutest dimples
  You are slender and very quiet
The display of your sweet disposition
  Made you special in my sight

I missed your early years
  But it didn't keep away
The tender love I felt for you
  When I met you *just today*

It was an unexpected pleasure
  The first time that we met
To find the sweetest great granddaughter
  A great grandmother could hope to get
10.25.07

Dedicated to my great granddaughter, Kaylee Taylor. (Kaylee is the daughter of my granddaughter, Alicia Holcomb Taylor (1973-2000), and granddaughter of my oldest son, Donald). Wow! And my oldest son is now the great grandfather of Lilyanne Hug Fairchild, Joshua Allen Fairchild and Daniel Fairchild (in 2012) That makes me a great-great grandmother...When did I get old enough to vote?

MICHAEL...
My All-Round Guy

Winsome and clever and loving a challenge
He is that rough and tumble all-round guy
Competent to accomplish all his goals in life
Anything he sets his mind to try

He tackles every obstacle
With insurmountable zeal
Challenging the opposing teams
Consistently on the football field

He is my real-life Texas cowboy
Full of amazing never-ending surprises
Not in all my wildest dreams did I
Anticipate his astonishing enterprises

He accepted a real life challenge
A young boy raising cattle
Wrestling with a thousand-pound stocker
Such an adventurous, formidable battle

He has proven to be dependable
Raising chickens, dogs and goats
Real masculine-macho – not a little whim
Nor a boy just sewing some "wild oats"
Continued

Certainly I am very proud of him
He's an industrious, conscientious guy
I know he will aspire to lofty heights
Reaching every ambition he resolves to try

No impasse ever frightens him
His fortitude is beyond compare
I pray that God will richly bless him
And keep him always in His care
08.22.10

Dedicated to my great grandson, Michael Taylor who has a intrepid spirit. He has, from the beginning of his life, already faced many challenges. My aspiration for him is for God to continue to keep him and bless him in every way. (Michael is the only son of my granddaughter Alicia Taylor, (1973-2000) who is the second daughter my of my eldest son, Donald).

DEUTERONOMY 6:5

"...And you shall love the Lord
your God
with all your heart and
with all your soul and
with all your might..."

ELIZABETH CHILD...
My Bright-Eyed Little Girl

I wrote a poem about your mom
   Your uncles and cousins, too
I wondered what I would write
   About a girl as sweet as you

Elizabeth, Elizabeth, bright-eyed little girl
   You have such a winsome smile
It makes me want to hug and hold you
   In my arms a little while

You have such sweetness
   And loving tenderness
So fascinating you are to me
   My precious little "Miss"

You are definitely very smart
   You love to sing and dance
And I would love to watch you skate
   As you twirl around and prance
07.07.07

Dedicated to my adorable little great granddaughter, Elizabeth Child, (Elizabeth is the daughter of Sandra Holcomb Child and granddaughter of my youngest son, David).

MATTHEW 6:22

"...The lamp of the body
Is the eye;
if therefore your eye
is clear,
your whole body
will be full of light..

ELIZABETH CHILD...
My Little Green-eyed Princess

In a soft, white frock
Prissy and lacy
You're a tiny, little princess
Light-hearted and racy

With sparkling green eyes
And pony-tail hair
You pose a confident spirit
And majestic, queenly flair

Slightly rumpled dress
A shiny little nose
Rosy-colored cheeks
You make a striking pose

When rollicking with laughter, or
Exemplifying a coy smile
Are you a scampering little elf
Or merely an enchanting child?
Continued

A buzz of conversation
Romping about in play
Perfectly at ease
In your child-like way

From grandfather's pockets
You pulled out all you could
The only toys you'd play with
Were grandfather's pocket goods

But he gladly let you
What else could he do?
You're a captivating princess
And he is in love with you
02.25.10

Dedicated to Elizabeth Child, my adorable great grand daughter. (Elizabeth is the daughter of my granddaughter Sandra Holcomb Child and she is my youngest son, David's granddaughter). Elizabeth radiates with the same love and gentleness that her mother, Sandra, has always portrayed.

CHRISTOPHER...
You Have Great Potential

I watched you run and play
   Growing taller every day
Your smile completely captivating
   My heart in every way

There' nothing more delightful
   Than the bright eyes of a child
Scampering -- running round and round
   Sporting your impish little smile

Looking to get into mischief
   Seeking new things to find
Flitting from place to place
   What do you have in mind?

I wonder what you will grow up to be
   Will you discover something new?
Or will you go to places still unknown?
   No matter what -- we'll be proud of you

You have a such a great potential
   To do great and mighty things
The world will be your oyster
   As success to you it brings

Go strive toward your highest goal
   And let God help you with the rest
May God bless you, my little cherub
   And may God grant you all the best
07.07.07

Dedicated to my little great grandson, Christopher Child. (Christopher is the son of my granddaughter Sandra Holcomb Child, and my youngest son, David's grandson). Christopher delights me in every way and I want God's best for him always as he fulfils his life's plan.

GRACE...
The Apple of My Eye

My adorable little princess-girl
You're growing up so fast
Time is flying by like whirlwinds
And your childhood's speeding past

You are such a precious child
I love your beautiful eyes
With your precocious little smile
You're such a treasured prize

Your eyes sparkle bright and twinkle
Like the stars up in the sky
Your sweet smile is mesmerizing
And you are the apple of my eye

You have a gentle disposition
Portraying kind acts of love
In every way you excite me
You're a blessing from God above

You delight in the world around you
Elated by all you see and do
You bring joy to everyone you meet
Just because you are -- just *you*

I love you, little princess-girl
And want the best of life for you
May God watch over you throughout life
Wherever you go...whatever you do
02.19.08

Dedicated to my great granddaughter, Grace Holcomb, (Grace is
the daughter of my only grandson, Casey Wayne Holcomb, who
is the son of my #3 son, David Holcomb). Grace is destined for
great things because of the love and kindness she portrays in all
of her ways and life. Sweetness and love flow from her like a
rushing river.

ANDREW...
Little Blue-Eyed Prince

Little blue-eyed prince
With golden locks so fine
I can not resist you when
Your hand slips into mine

Little fingers tugging
To go see what is there
Inquisitive and winsome
You're not afraid to dare

Unyielding curiosity
Exploring all around
Sometimes it incites annoyance
But temptation *does* abound

Go look into the toy box
See what it has in store
Big red balls await you
Other toys loom there galore

But that's never good enough
For this little prince, you see
He only wants to play
With things that belong to *me!*
03.30.09

Dedicated to Andrew Holcomb, my great grandson. (Andrew is the son of my only grandson, Casey Wayne Holcomb and the grandson of my youngest son, David). Andrew is my final opportunity for "great-grandmother-hood," Andrew is a most inquisitive child. He is destined for vast amazing adventures. *My* next adventure is "great-great grandmother-hood." I can't wait!

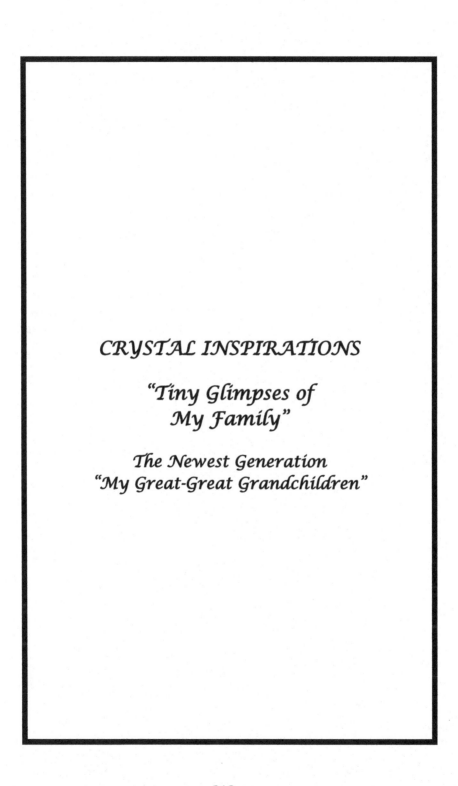

CRYSTAL INSPIRATIONS

"Tiny Glimpses of
My Family"

The Newest Generation
"My Great-Great Grandchildren"

She is growing
So fast

FOR MY FIRST
GREAT-GREAT GRANDCHILD
Lilyanne Grace Hug Fairchild

JOSHUA
ALLEN
FAIRCHILD

Minutes old

FIRST GREAT-GREAT GRAND SON
Oh boy, is he a feisty one; he slipped in
under the publisher's deadline
Born 09-17-10

No picture yet of little Daniel Fairchild...He's
coming...Number three Great-Great.

MATTHEW 18:3

"...Truly I Say unto you, unless you are converted and become like children, you shall not enter the kingdom of heaven..."

A BABY IS COMING

Her tummy is growing
With baby inside
A child is coming
Its parent's pride

A babe's coming
But we know not who
Which shall I buy
Either pink or blue?

The babe is coming
Now this is a test
When you are deciding
Which color is best

I think when buying
A neutral should do
Then it will please
Regardless who

Quick -- the babe is coming!
Now what shall I do?
Time is a-wasting, well...
Guess it's "yellow" for you!
07.19.08

KNOW WHAT I WISH FOR YOU?
My First Great-Great Grandchild
Lilyanne

Know what I wish for you?
The best things there are
Each day to be for you
Your nicest thus far

And happiness always
Because you're finally here
And more of the same
Throughout every coming year

Congratulations on the day of your birth
Lilyanne
06.04.09

Dedicated to my first great-great grandchild, Lilyanne Grace Hug Fairchild. (Lilyanne is the daughter of my great grandson, Benjamin Fairchild, who is the son of Amy LaNette Holcomb Fairchild, my first granddaughter. Amy, is now a grandmother herself; thereby, making me a double-great grandmother and making Amy's father, my #1 son, Donald Holcomb, a young, great-grandfather!) Wow! I seem to be getting "older and greater!"

PROVERBS 22:6

"...train up a child in the way
He should go, even when he is old
He will not depart from it..."

A PRECIOUS NEW ARRIVAL

A baby coming is so exciting
A new life has just begun
I know that you are happy
To have this special son

As you watch him grow
New adventures for you have begun
With each breaking day he will
Learn to smile and sing and run

Keep your eyes wide open
Years pass before you think
Many things you'll miss
If you even stop to blink

Fill his days with laughter
It's medicine beyond compare
When hard times come his way
It will keep him from despair
Continued

218

You cannot spoil a little boy
With too many hugs or kisses
A little boy is spoiled
By loving things he misses

An encouraging word, a tender touch
That's what this boy will need
To grow into a fine, young man
And make you proud, indeed

We will all be watching him
Grow from baby, boy to man
Our hearts will grow with love for him
As he develops within God's plan
07.07.10

Dedicated to my newest great-great grandchild, Joshua. (Joshua
is the son of my great-grandson, Kirk Fairchild, who is the oldest
son of my granddaughter, Amy Holcomb Fairchild and great
grandson of my #1 son, Donald).. Oops, oh boy, is he ever a
feisty one. He slipped in under the publisher's deadline. Joshua
Allen Fairchild, born 09.17.10, my first great-great grandson.
Welcome little Joshua.

THERE'S ANOTHER ONE COMING

Another great-great grandchild is coming
This time another boy it's said to be
I know this little great-great
Will be a terrific joy for me

What am I to think?
Am I getting this old and gray?
It seems only yesterday I was a little girl
Who went out in the yard to play

Was that little girl really me?
Or was that just my dreams?
Really I couldn't be getting *this* old
At least it's not the way it seems

Well life keeps on passing by
New generations will tell the tale
I suppose now I must admit to getting old
Since wrinkles and gray hair I can't curtail
Continued

Continued

Getting old grants me a few privileges
Like wearing purple with a red hat
Doing lots of things I couldn't do before
And they let me get away with that

It's good to know that life goes on
And new pages will be turned
Little great-greats will keep coming along
And their own place in life they'll earn

Well little boy for you I am waiting
To see what you will be and do
I pray your life will always be blessed
However I'm already proud of you
02.02.12

Dedicated to already named, Daniel Fairchild, son of my
grandson Benjamin. Daniel has not arrived yet. My third great-
great grandchild is on the way. I'm becoming a greater great-great
rapidly.

RING OUT THE BELLS

Ring out the bells
For this special event
Happiness today
To a young couple is sent

A new little babe
About to be born
Great pride on the faces
Of the parents is worn

Hoping and waiting
Yearning, it's true
Now ring out the bells
A babe awaits you
02.02.12

Dedicated to Daniel Fairchild, about to be born. (Daniel is the second child of my great grandson Benjamin and the grandson of my granddaughter, Amy. He is the great grandson of my #1 Son, Donald. That makes him my #3 great-great grandchild). My bells are ringing joyously...life goes on.

GROWTH

I'm just a tiny, little pecan
A sittin' in a tree
Someday I'll fall down
Then something else I'll be

I'll lie upon the ground
'Til I start to sprout, you see
Then as soon as I am ready
I'll become a great, strong tree

The winds will blow around me
The rains will come and go
My leaves will begin to sprout
And little pecans will start to show

The process starts all over again
Little pecans falling from my tree
Those little pecans will grow, then they .
Become great, strong trees...like me
Then life repeats, repeats
repeats
08.01.02

Dedicated to all my kids, grandkids, great grandkids and the
great-great grandkids to come that are springing up like little
pecans all over the place. It is my hope that they will all become
strong, beautiful men and women...(just like me).

CRYSTAL INSPIRATIONS

"Tiny Glimpses of
My Family"

On Loan from Emery
Via Marriage
Grand and Great Grandchildren

JOHN HATHAWAY...
My Little Charmer

So full of mischief
But all just in fun
You're a genuine boy
Our precious grandson

I cannot resist
The charm of your smile
Or the warmth of your arms
When you hold me a while

I'm always delighted
By your winsome ways
You are a real charmer
Like a breath of spring days

You're an all-round athlete
Who's as smart as can be
So full of imagination
And prodding curiosity

I'm always happy
To see your bright face
You have gained in my heart
A most special place

So wherever you go
And whatever you do
Please remember, dear grandson
Grandmother Tuttle loves you
12.24.78

Dedicated to my "big" little charmer, John Frederic Hathaway, Emery's grandson (on loan to me via marriage). Thank you John for your unconditional love. I am proud of you (in 2012) and your four precious happy little children, who are also mine (on loan to me via marriage).

JOSEPH HATHAWAY...
My Little Cherub

You're like a little cherub
  Snuggling on a cloud
Our darling little grandson
  Who really makes me proud

You are very tenderhearted
  Compassionate and kind
Yet you're a tough and tumble boy
  Who has mischief on his mind

Sometimes you're like a pixie
  Scampering here and there
Or maybe like a gentle breeze
  Without a worldly care

I know you have strong muscles
  They grow stronger every day
You can do 'most anything
  When you go out to play

I love to feel your little arms
  Squeezing me e'er so tight
You give the sweetest kisses
  Your smiles are sunny-bright

So my little cherub
  Stay kind and sweet and true
Always keep in mind
  Grandmother Tuttle loves you
12.24.78

Dedicated to our little grandson, Joseph Michael Hathaway,
Emery's Grandson (on loan to me via marriage). Joseph, you are
always happy to see me. I love you bunches. May God richly
bless you.

ELIZABETH

EMILY

JONATHAN

JOSHUA

THE HATHAWAYS
MY GREAT GRANDCHILDREN BY MARRIAGE
(CHILDREN OF EMERY'S GRANDSON, JOHN HATHAWAY)

YOUR SMILES

Your smiles spread sunshine
And people can see and know
The Christ-likeness in you
That your sunny smiles do show

Your smiles stretch out
Touching people far and near
Your smiles allow people to see
That our God is really here
02.28.83

Dedicated to four happy Hathaway children. They make every visit with them a cheerful and delightful time. I'm glad I get to enjoy them via marriage to Emery. My blessings to each one of you. Smile and the world smiles with you.

ELIZABETH HATHAWAY...
Sweet As Honey

My sweet as honey little girl
You're growing up so fast my head
Is accelerated into a spinning whirl

You have a beautiful face and eyes
And your adorable personality displays
A sweetness crammed with a surprise

A cute and charming little girl
Your heart's so full of love it makes
You priceless like the rarest pearl

You're an enthralling child
As vivacious as a summer's breeze
A girl who can always make me smile
02.19.10

Dedicated to Elizabeth Hathaway, my sweet and loving great granddaughter (on loan from Emery via marriage). (She's the oldest daughter of Emery's grandson, John Hathaway). She is filled with love for God and love for others. She's a very, very smart young lady with a smile that is as warm as sunshine. Elizabeth, you inherited your great grandfather Emery's kind and loving spirit...always maintain your sweet spirit.

EMILY HATHAWAY...
Embracing Life

You are a precocious little wall-climber
Spontaneous with tremendous imagination
There are no feats too daring
To make you show fear or hesitation

You have the antics of a monkey
Yet you are as gentle as a lamb
And you have the prowess of the lion
As you climb the bathroom door jamb

You will walk along the high porch rail
You're not afraid to climb the tallest tower
With your dauntless, fearless spirit
Nothing is out of your reach or power

You are as agile as a honey bee
Flitting from flower to flower
You twist and turn and jump around
Dancing gracefully hour after hour
Continued

Dazzling as a priceless diamond
Sparkling like the evening star
You have a marvelous mystique
A fascinating little girl you are

You have a flair all your own
So provocative and exhilarating
You do all sorts of incredible things
My heart you are quickly captivating

You have flirty, flirty eyes and a
Lighthearted charm that you can't hide
You are such a mesmerizing surprise
I'm filled with a delightful gush of pride
08.09.10

Dedicated to my flamboyant little great granddaughter, Emily Hathaway, (on loan from Emery via marriage). (She's the second daughter of Emery's grandson, John Hathaway.) She surprises and delights us with all her antics. She endears us with her abilities and charm us with her charismatic personality and loving disposition. These qualities, Emily, you inherited from your great grandfather Emery, don't ever lose them.

EMILY, EMILY...
Mischievous Child

I'm looking at your picture
I see mischief in your eyes
You are planning to do something
That will be a big surprise

I'm not sure it will be approved
By mother, dad or me
But we will have to wait
For what antics we will see

You might climb the bathroom wall
Or jump off a high porch rail
Whatever you have planned
We can never tell

You are so adorable
When your exploits materialize
However we dare not laugh at you
'Cause there's mischief in your eyes
Continued

Our laughter just encourages you
To do one more audacious thing or two
So we dare not show how much we like
The cute things that you do

You're growing up so fast now
These adventures may soon die down
But I believe that in your heart
You will always be that clown

Hopefully your adventurous spirit
Will never fade away
Throughout your life you'll stay bold
And courageous in every way
02.18.08

Dedicated to my great-granddaughter Emily Hathaway (on loan via marriage), the cutest little wall-climber I've ever seen. Emily, your great-great grandmother, Clara Tuttle, joined the circus when she was a young lady of twenty-five. She was the "Goddess of Liberty" in the Ringling Brothers Barnum & Bailey Circus, riding atop the lion's cage in the circus parade. You have inherited her adventurous genes and your great grandfather Emery's loving adventurous spirit. Don't ever lose your inheritance.

JONATHAN HATHAWAY...
With an Inquisitive Mind

There is no limit for the possibilities
For a boy with an inquisitive mind
Adventure is always in his heart
There's no telling what he will find

He keeps asking critical questions
Discarding all the useless details
Challenging all the given facts
Searching until the truth it tells

What will he accomplish
Searching the unknown?
Will he find new things in space, or
Discover breakthrough feats at home?

Will he climb lofty mountains?
Or scan the deep blue sea?
No matter what he aspires to do
A success I'm sure he'll be

Wherever he chooses to venture
Whatever he determines to do
He must remember the wisest discovery
Is knowing God must always lead you
09.01.10

Dedicated to Jonathan Hathaway, my inquisitive great-grandson
(on loan from Emery via marriage). Jonathan has a million
questions and is not afraid to endeavor to try and do new things.
He is full of adventure. He's like his great grandfather Emery, who
built our two-story house by himself at age 71; and earned his
private pilot's license at age 76 ,and flew his own plane until age
88! Jonathan, I hope you retain your great grandfather's
audacious spirit always, it's your inheritance.

JOSHUA HATHAWAY...
With the Sweetest Hugs and Kisses

It is amazing the power
Of your heart-felt embrace
And how far reaching your hug can go
They reached my deepest place

You give the warmest hugs
And the sweetest kisses, too
The love you emanate
Is love that's really true

Your love radiates a candor
That cannot be dismissed
It's portrayed by your every hug
And expressed in your every kiss

With your wide-eyed innocence
Whenever you take a notion
You reveal a little pixie
With perpetual motion

You are a brilliant little boy
With a vivid curiosity
You attack every exploit
With high-speed velocity
Continued

236

I see your bright eyes twinkling
A mischievous grim is upon your face
Are you embarking on a new discovery, or
Headed on a voyage to some exotic place?

You are fascinating and exciting
With an acute inquisitive mind
You embrace all of life's mysteries
Always eager new discoveries to find

You are unforgettable and extraordinary
I know you'll grow into a fine young man
Destiny has great things in store for you
Your life's in God's greatest plan
07.07.10

Dedicated to Joshua Hathaway, my lovable little great grandson. Every time you reach up to hug and kiss me, my heart melts. I'm so glad you are mine (on loan from Emery via marriage). You inherited your great grandfather Emery's sweet, gentle, forgiving temperament.

CRYSTAL INSPIRATIONS

"Spotlighting Friends"

MY BEST FRIEND

When I choose a best friend
I want one just like you
Because I know you'll love me
And will always be true-blue

We always laugh together
We play and drink a bit
But everything we do is
A genuine bona "fineable" hit!

I'm glad you are my friend
And I wanted you to know
I love you very much
I want my love to show
07.04.10

MILLIONS and BILLIONS
Of Thank Yous

I cannot thank you enough
for all the things you do so
I am sending you millions and billions
of tons of love
and millions and billions
of baskets of thankfulness

I am giving these to you
with my heartfelt affection
along with millions and billions
of hugs and kisses
but millions and billions aren't sufficient
to thank you my dear, dear friend

08.18.10

I NEED A FRIEND
Who Will Stand By Me

There are times I must walk my path alone
Other times a need a friend to stand by me
A friend who is trustworthy
Whose honesty exhibits steadfast integrity

A friend who knows God in all His glory
And will walk a lonely path with me
Motivating and inspiring me along each step
Even when the outcome we cannot see

I need a friend who brings sunshine into my life
One whose smile cheers me on to victory
Regardless how hard or long the struggle
I know that friend is there for me

A friend whose love never fades nor dwindles
Who walks beside me along the narrow way
Whose compassion and concern sustains me
And helps me as I struggle through another day

I need a friend who points me to the living God
Encouraging me to trust and obey only Him today
Because a friend like that will truly bless me
And will help me find God's perfect way
07.17.10

THE GOOD NEWS

When you feel discouraged
And you begin to have the blues
Look for the good around you
And listen for good news

When you see the bad
Or hear words that are unkind
Let them pass unnoticed
So they can never undermine

Discouragement will only flourish
If much attention it is given
Render it helpless by neglect
Let the blues from you be driven
10.04.71

PROVERBS 17:17; 22

*"A friend loveth at all times...
A merry heart does good like
a medicine..."*

THINKING ABOUT YOU TODAY

I was thinking about you today
Remembering the laughs shared along the way
The times together when things were tough
We laughed and cried through all that stuff
We've been friends for many years

You were there for me and I for you
We're friends forever with a friendship true
Even though we live far apart
You will always be in my heart
We've shared our joys; we've cried salty tears
08.31.08

Dedicated to Aline Cole with whom I've been friends for nearly 60
years. Friendships last. And I dedicate this to friendship. To have
a friend, you must be a friend.

MY APPRECIATION

Sometimes I take it for granted
In the rush of what I do
I forget to say a "thank you"
For the wonderful things you do

I really appreciate
All the efforts you put out
I want to just say "thank you"
That's what this note's about

This does not really say enough but
Thank you, thank you, thank you again
You are very special to me
My thoughtful and very good friend
02.02.09

I'M CALLING YOU
RING-A-LING, DING-A-LING

Ring-a-ling, ding-a-ling
How are you, my dear
Ring-a-ling, ding-a-ling
Are you planning to be there

We have an extraordinary speaker
She has exciting tales to tell
It will be a wonderful time
Hearing the stories she'll dispel

Now, dear, if you can't be there
This is the time to say
If you wait to cancel later
For your lunch you still must pay

Well I'll say good-bye for now
We're glad you're coming, dear
Always we all look forward
To seeing everybody there

Your Telephone Reservation Committee
Cedar Creek Lake Women's Club
04.27.10

Notation: While I was serving on the Cedar Creek women's Club
I wrote many greeting cards for the club. This is a sample of one
of them.

FRIENDSHIP

There's nothing about time
That will make a true friend
You can know some forever
And their friendships not win

The first time I met you
A new friendship we made
True friendship forever
Our friendship won't fade

The test of a friendship
As you plainly can see
Is not how many times
You will visit with me

Many times I won't see you
But the times that I do
I know that our friendship
Will always be true

A friendship's not measured
I am sure that you know
By the money that's spent
Or what treasures you show

You might spend a fortune
Or not even a dime
It's not spending money
But it's how you spend time
Continued

Some think words can express
A true friendship's intent
But **just** words can not say
What truly is meant

Words can only express
Just a very small part
When you try to explain what
You feel in your heart

Our friendship thus far
Is of short duration
We've had little time
For much visitation

But I don't want love measured
By how much time we have spent
And words aren't trustworthy
Because they can be bent

Some believe this might mean
Our friendship's not strong
But I tell you the truth
They would be ever so wrong

Our friendship can endure
It can always be true
If you show love for me
And I show love for you
05.18.06

ALONE

I saw her again today
How thin she looked -- how frail
Sitting alone, staring into space
Auras of sadness prevail

Her face drawn in hopelessness
Marked by years of discontent
Too late to change that path now
The effect shall n'er relent

A vicious malady with wretchedness
Assaults her very life and breath
Without conciliation or relief
Unmercifully incessant unto death

Long ago she set her path
Sought not a single friend
Now sick and sad, bent and frail
Alone she must face life's end

She did not seem to comprehend
Friendship's special value
Foregoing comfort and compassion
And what friendship's love could do

My heart aches now for her
As her life nears to its end
Yet that day I spoke not -- nor she
For I knew her not as "friend"
07.01.79

Notation: One day, I observed a UTHSCD employee sitting alone. I had never taken time to get to know her. I heard she had been diagnosed with terminal cancer. I don't remember her name. It makes me sad that I never tried to get to know her. She could have used a friend.

BEST FRIENDS

I'm revealing a component of me
That only few have seen
A part that's hidden deep inside
And this is what I mean

Private thoughts, words and deeds
Within my heart I've sealed
Only to my very best friend
Would I these things reveal

Because we are connected
Like a circle without end
That's what makes it special
About being a very best friend

Our friendship is never ending
It's complete -- within, without
We surely are best friends
Of this there is no doubt
03.01.96

WISHING YOU A NICE DAY

Wishing you a special day
That's happy through and through
Because there could never be
A day too nice for you
03.04.04

HAPPY FRIENDSHIP DAY

SPIRITUAL COMPANIONS

We break the Bread of Life together
   At the Table of our Lord
We sip His Living Water
   And feast upon His Word

Mutually sharing life's experiences
   Hand-in-hand we walk along
Under the care of God's great mercy
   We unite in spiritual song

To inspire, encourage and challenge
   When one of us becomes forlorn
Our deepest feelings we can share
   Without any fear of scorn

Our spirits are richly nurtured
   Through the counsel of a friend
We are bid to resist temptations
   And stand steadfast unto the end

The bonds of love are strengthened
   'Til we're more than partner-friend
As we are rooted in God's Spirit
   Our souls solidify and blend

But it's more than just companions
   Sharing our lives hand-in-hand
We together share God's presence
   And seek His perfect plan
10.11.84

Dedicated to my spiritual inspiration, companion, mentor, friend,
Crystal Elliott.

WE TOUCHED

Core-to-core
    Life-to-life -- we touched
    Unyielding to any freedom lost

Wholly me
    Wholly you -- we touched
    Increasing our eagerness for more life

Me-to-you
    You-to-me -- we touched
    Pointing each other toward eternal things

All-of-me
    All-of-you -- was touched
    Shaping and enriching our individual value

More-of-me
    More-of-you -- was touched
    Deepening our awareness of God

Core-to-core
    Life-to-life -- we were touched as we
    Gave God praise for our friendship
11.20.84

Dedicated to the one friend who has most significantly and inspirationally touched my life, Crystal Elliott .As our friendship deepened, I was drawn closer to God through her inspiration and friendship. Thank you, Lord, for the blessing of friends.

MY CONTAGIOUS FRIEND

You're someone's favorite sister-in-law
Someone's favorite mother-in-law, too
The favorite wife, mother, teacher, friend
To many others who have known you

You are also my favorite friend
But to me where you excel the best
You're my favorite "Christian" example
Alongside Paul and John and all the rest

You are contagious, my friend
More than any other girl or boy
And I keep catching you
Because you have contagious "joy"
01.01.84

Dedicated to my favorite Christian friend, inspiration and Christian
example, who is full of the "joy of the Lord -- Crystal Elliott.
Beware – because she is contagious!

WISHING YOU HAPPINESS

A special, loving thought
I send to you today
Just a note to keep in touch

With a friend who is dear to me
Know that your friendship
Means so very, very much
01.03.10

RICHARD S.A. TINDALL, M.D.
My Neighbor

Since my poems have just made you smile
I'll write one for you but it may take a while
Even though there's really a lot I could say
I don't have time to do it today

Do you want me to tell all about your best side?
Or should I reveal what you're trying to hide?
You're tall and handsome; this much I'll claim
And probably your research will lead you to fame

But stuff like that is too hard to rhyme
Listing your "good" points takes too much time
This poem will be short, but not 'cause I'm lazy
The phones are ringing and driving me crazy

I've known you now for quite a long while
The best part about you I like -- is your *smile*
I guess the last thing I'll say in your favor
For a *guy*, not too bad...and you're a nice neighbor
01.18.78

Dedicated to Richard S.A. Tindall. M.D., UTHSCD
Co-worker, doctor, friend, whose office was next to mine.

DOCTOR TINDALL...
My "Potty-Stall" Doctor

Although I would be the last to say
You really were a good friend today
When I was in such an awkward position
You came immediately to be my physician

Scalding hot coffee is not good, nor "fun"
Especially if down your leg it does run
You must agree I was indisposed
Sitting there with my legs all exposed

Exposed legs I could surely endure
At my age they have very little allure
But "*in the john*" really blitzed me out
It is so disconcerting; there is no doubt

Many doctors would make a simple house call
But who could you get for a "potty-stall-call?"
Most docs would think you were delirious
They wouldn't believe you were really serious
Continued

254

I thought about which doctor to take
For this peculiar call they must make
Deliver me from a lot of harassment
I couldn't stand much more embarrassment

To each of you doctors, I'd like to be fair
But I can choose only one for my primary care
I know you think this was probably a plot
Really...Tindall's name...**I drew right out of**
 ...the pot!
06.13.78

Dedicated to Richard S.A. Tindall, M.D., one of the numerous
doctors I worked with at UTHSCD. But, he was the only doctor I
trusted to be my "potty-stall-doctor" when I spilled scalding hot
coffee in my lap and he had to come into the girls' potty-stall to
attend to my burned exposed legs, etc., etc.

COFFEE CAN COMA

You came by our office
Just the other day
To pick up some coffee
And be on your way

You were unsuspecting
Of the event to come
It was incredible
The thing that was done

Little did I realize
How powerful I am
Or with how much vigor
And strength I abound

I glanced at you slightly
And thought to myself
I'll pitch him some coffee
Right off of this shelf
Continued

How could I know
You have no dexterity
Considering your cleverness
What caused that disparity?

So I pitched the coffee
It went straight to your head
From the excruciating pain
You thought you were dead

As you were leaving
I heard you expound
I get "coffee can coma"
Every time I come 'round!
07.26.78

Dedicated to Isaac Crawford, M.D., V.A. Hospital, Dallas, Texas,
the first "Coffee Can Coma" patient...not really -- just a little poetic
license. But, I did hit him in the head with a can of coffee.
Sorry...!

THE LOOK OF THE EAGLE

With assurance and self-confidence
The eagle soars through the skies
Lofting toward the highest peak
Each motion synchronized

Rising far above the usual
No ordinary bounds he knows
With grand and haughty maneuvers
Great expertise he shows

The eagle's noted for sharp vision
With alert and piercing eyes
He surveys his whole domain
As he swoops down from the skies

He's the emblem of the ancient Roman
And the symbol of our nation
His strength and power attest to
Why he excites such admiration
Continued

To the Indian the feat of greatness
Was to reach the eagle's nest
To wear the eagle's feather
Was the sign he passed his test

The mighty eagle does not live
In the shadow of anyone
He exhibits no fear of any foe
With valor his struggle's won

He's a graceful and majestic figure
With an exhilarating fascination
Always spiraling upwards
Captivating the imagination

You have that "Look of the Eagle"
A success in every way
Endowed with a dauntless spirit
To great things you'll aspire some day
10.17.78

Dedicated to Jay W. Pettegrew, M.D., UTHSCD, physician, co-worker and friend and to the success of his research ventures.

A TRIBUTE

Oh, yeah! To a great man -- a tribute
Yet that greatness was carried lightly
With little account made of honors, yet
His gratitude was undeniably manifested

He occupies numerous positions of honor
Going easily about them with faithfulness
Quietly displaying a decorum of mannerism
Attesting to his inner strength

He is neither ungracious, nor remote
Although not prone to be demonstrative
He possesses a capacity to disregard himself
Yet a brilliant breadth of knowledge is retained

Within the greatness of this man
Abides the ability to remain human
Language cannot capture his essence
Nor the depth of feelings brought forth by him

Already bestowed with many honors
Which were worn with humility
There remains no need to dwell longer upon
His greatness -- for his genius is transparent
05.01.79

Dedicated to R. Malcolm Stewart, M.D., UTHSCD, in appreciation
for his research in Parkinson, Huntington and other neurological
diseases.

"LIPTON, HERE"

Gosh, it's such a pleasure
To greet your cheery smile
Or just hear your pleasant voice
With its "English style"

"Lipton, here," you say
When I call you on the phone
A smile is in your voice and
Happiness in your tone

I like to call you up
Just to chat a while
'Cause your warm and happy voice
Makes my whole day smile

When I'm feeling blue
And need a little cheer
I'll call you on the phone
For your greeting, "Lipton, here"
02.21.79

Dedicated to James Lipton, M.D.,UTHSCD, whose thermo-
chemistry works perfectly, making him such a pleasant, warm-
hearted creature.

261

THE LEGEND CALLED
Nurse Near

An infectious smile she has
   Spreading from ear to ear
This is the beginning
   Of the legend called Nurse Near

She's not a super star
   But she tackles all of life
With her indomitable spirit
   That drives away all strife

Sunshine spreads around her
   As giggles from her spill
She's really like a little kid
   With a hundred dollar bill

In a world of sour apples
   She's as priceless as a peach
She brings happiness to all around
   And brightens the day of each

If you're wearing an awful frown
   And need a bit of cheer
Listen for the giggling
   Of the legend called Nurse Near
01.20.81

Dedicated to Nurse Lisa Near, UTHSCD, the nurse with the cutest giggle you will ever hear. Laughter is the best medicine.

PROVERBS 17:22

"...A joyful heart does good
Like a medicine,..."

OUR SECRET

Shhhhhhhhhhhhhhhh...

Shhhhhhhhhhhhhhhh...
A secret, a secret, a secret we share
But don't get despondent; don't even despair
Your secret is safe down deep in my heart
It will never get out; no rumor will start

Shhhhhhhhhhhhhhhh...
Although accidentally it was stumbled upon
What I found out will never be known
Until **you** are ready the news to spread 'round
No one from me will hear even a sound

Shhhhhhhhhhhhhhhh...
I'll be quiet as a mouse; and that is a fact
Spreading rumors 'round; why I have more tact
Upon my word you can truly depend
I won't let you down; I'll be a good friend
Shhhhhhhhhhhhhhhh
01.10.78

Notation: The secret is out -- Ursela Newdeck is getting married.
Shhhhhhhhhhhhhhhh...! Dedicated to Ursela Newdeck and
congratulations on your marriage that we all know about, now
Shhhhhhhhhhhhhhhh...!

SUDDENLY---
A HAPPENING

Today was a day like you'd never believe
A sight for sore eyes like you rarely would see

Pat was trotting down the middle of the street
Prissy and prancing with high-stepping feet

Suddenly when everything else seemed all right
The look on Pat's face said she was "a-fright"

You never would guess what happened that day
Her raggedy breeches in place would not stay

Before she knew it her drawers had slipped down
And that was the reason she wore such a frown

Now she'll believe what her mother once said
Wearing raggedy breeches will turn your face red

What purpose had she for her choice on that morn
She knew raggedy panties should never be worn

We think she wanted for us to know this one fact
She wears "white" panties, although she is "black"
04.06.78

Dedicated to my sweet, lovely black friend, Pat Smith, co-worker, UTHSCD, and based on a true happening. Pat was headed across the street for lunch, when suddenly the elastic on her "panties" broke and they fell to the ground. She had been warned about wearing worn-out breeches, but paid no mind to the counsel from her dear mom. What a revolting state of affairs that was!

EVERY LIFE IS UNIQUE

Every life is unique
Each life is an extraordinary tale
But no matter how much you plan
The outcome you cannot foretell

Circumstance can change the pattern
To different shapes or colors or other
One person touches your life one way
There are different touches by another

Who can know what time has in store
Disasters can shape life's decisions
And changes are made by life's successes
Even events stacked together cause revisions

Some moments rush by us
Like lightening in the sky
Other moments take their time
The reasons we don't know why

All our thoughts and actions
Are absorbed into our memory
And linger until they are totally
Embedded into life's symmetry

Each life becomes unique
By its patterns and design
Each life develops into the whole
By our choices and by time
01.22.10

YOUR INFECTIOUS LAUGH

Remember when I asked you
On that little self-quiz test
Which feature about yourself
Do you really like the best?

The first thing that you mentioned
You guessed it was your eyes
And since they are quite pretty
It came as no surprise

Of course you can not hear yourself
As others hear your voice
But if I did the pickin'
Your laugh would be my choice

Your laugh is so infectious
It spreads to all around
It has a hint of sensualism
With a pleasant lingering sound

It is impossible to describe it
It's sensual and so passionate
But it has a little hint of mischief
Yet warmhearted and compassionate

It is not a robust bellow
Nor a crackling sound
It is provocative and exciting
Still a certain mystique is found

But if you still insist
Your eyes are your best feature
Then teach your eyes your infectious laugh
That'd make you a super-duper teacher!!!!
08.03.78

OVER AND OVER AGAIN

I see your dress is different today
You really should change it every day
  Over
    And over
      Again
Yesterday you put us to the test
You wore that same old yesterday's dress
  Over
    And over
      Again
I'm sure you want to look your best
But must it be in the same old dress?
  Over
    And over
      Again
Don't you care what people think?
That same old dress will start to stink
  Over
    And over
      Again
Don't you realize people will know
When you don't change before you go?
  Over
    And over
      Again
Since you've repented, we'll let it pass
But don't wear this dress like you did the last
  Over
    And over
      Again
        08.03.78

It's a good thing it's your birthday Denise, or I would have written a tacky poem. Dedicated to Denise Wernet, co-worker and friend, UTHSCD, who spent the night with a friend then had to wear the same dress to work the next day again...oops!

THE DAY I SET FIRE
TO OUR PRIVY

It is time I was bold
and tell the tale I've not told
of the day I set fire
to our PRIVY!

My sweet little sis
was so tiny a miss
she would fall through the hole
in that PRIVY!

I had such a dread fear
we would lose the poor dear
I begged daddy, please fix
that old PRIVY!

But he just wouldn't hear
said, 'twas an unfounded fear
no one has **ever** been lost
in a PRIVY!

Since he'd not understand
I just took things in hand
and set out to burn down
that old PRIVY!

There is one thing -- or two
that my dad never knew
'bout the day of the fire
in our PRIVY!
Continued

269

I at last thought it best
that I finally confess
it was "*I*" who set fire
to our PRIVY!

To my momma, I said
all the guilt's on my head
I'm the one who burned down
our poor PRIVY!

Oh no, my dear, she cried out to me
that just could not possibly be
'twas the neighbors who set fire
to our PRIVY!

Once she thought me so bad
that no illness I had
but she could never blame **me**
for that PRIVY!

Well mothers believe
what they want to perceive
nonetheless -- **I did** set fire
to that PRIVY!
04.27.83

Dedicated to Mildred Sutleff, friend and resident of Silver Leaves
Nursing Home, Dallas, Texas. Based on the true story she told of
her little sister, Bessie Geraldine Dailey, who always fell through
the hole in their privy! Mildred set fire to their privy because her
father wouldn't fix it!

PSALM 51:17

*"...The sacrifices of God are a broken
Spirit; A broken and contrite heart
O God, Thou wilt not despise..."*

JOHN 15:13

*"...Greater love has no one than this,
that one lay down his life for
his friends..."*

PROVERBS 17:17

"...A friend Loves at all times..."

MY SPECIAL FRIEND
MARILYNNE

*You touched my life in a special way today
A dreary cloud was in my way
You helped me see the sun come through
And encouraged me to start anew*

*I'll remember you as a special friend
Who helped me let the sunshine in
Our Lord will bless you in every way
For representing Him as His child today*

*My life is brighter as you can see
Because of the love you've shown to me
I will always be your friend, too
A special friend -- one who deeply loves you*
02.15.94

Dedicated to Marilynne Barney, who has since gone home to be
with our Lord (2001), because she always loved and encouraged
me and made my days brighter and fuller and I miss her dearly.
She was a true friend in all her ways, totally faithful to friendship,
to family and to God.

MY SWEET HANNAH

With long blond hair
And big blue eyes
Looking everywhere
For her little surprise

You are full of joy
And sweet as honey
You're smart as a whip
Whimsical and funny

I love to watch you
When you sing and pray
And watch you grow sweeter
Each and every day

Such an adorable girl
I want you to know
I love you so much
I want my love to show
05.28.08

Dedicated to five-year-old Hannah Gowan who attends our church. She looks for the little surprise package I prepare for her each Sunday. She delights in everything she gets. I wrote her name on her package in Morse Code and gave her the key and showed her how to decipher the code. I asked her to figure out what I had written on her package using the key and tell me the following week what it meant. However, in just a few minutes, she sat down and figured out I had written her name in Morse Code. A few weeks later, she wrote a note to her mother in Morse Code using the key to construct it. She is a very smart little girl. My joy to know.

ADRIANA...
The Bright Eyes of A child

There's nothing as delightful
As the bright eyes of a child
Scampering 'round and 'round
Looking for her little surprise

Flitting from place to place
Looking for mischief to get into
Finding something hidden
In a secret place or two

A mischievous smile upon her face
Delight forming in her bright eyes
Suddenly in a little dark corner
A little surprise she spies
02.02.10

Dedicated to two-year-old Adriana Gowan who looks diligently every Sunday for her surprise package with such delight. She attends our church. Her favorite surprises are any kind of jewelry and chocolate candy.

MY LITTLE PUPPY
BEETHOVEN

He was so, so sweet
So, so cute
So very, very loveable

He laid beside me
He licked me kisses
He was so adorable

He jumped and played
He ran all day
He even danced with me

I moved away
I miss him so
I know he misses me

He quickly ate
He didn't growl
He loved me tenderly

A little dog
A special friend
A happy memory
06.10.79

Dedicated to our Irving, Texas, neighbor girl, Laura Brooks, in
memory of her puppy Beethoven. She had to leave him behind
when they moved to Irving.

MY LITTLE PUPPY
GERTRUDE

You have a so-so cuteness
   And you also have bad breath
      But you play with all my friends
     And me

You have so-so soft fur
   And you also have floppy ears
      but you sit by the table to eat
     By me

You have a so-so playfulness
   And you lick sticky-icky kisses
      But you do a so-so dance
     For me

You have a so-so bark
   And you growl at all the neighbors
      But you frequently take a bite
     Of me

You are kind of a so-so dog, Gertrude
   And you are kind of so-so cute
      But you are kind of so-so loved
     By me
06.10.79

Dedicated to Laura Brooks, our neighbor in Irving, Texas, and to her so-so doggie, Gertrude, who replaced Beethoven, the dog she loved and had to leave behind when they moved.

A TOUCH OF JOY

She was a little pixie girl
Warm-hearted and care-free
She brought a touch of joy
Into my life, you see

Sparkling with happiness
With expressive, big brown eyes
Exquisitely beautiful
A magnificent surprise

Innovated and imaginative
Kind and loving, she
A very special someone
Deeply touching me

Charming as a melodious bird
With a sweetness all its own
Or the sweet-scented fragrance
Made by the rose alone

Like a magnetic power
This unpretentious child
Infiltrated my heart
With her enchanting smile

Love ad infinitum
By choice I can enjoy
Because into my life
She brings a touch of joy
06.10.79

Dedicated to Laura Brooks, my little next door neighbor girl when
we lived in Irving, Texas, in 1979. She was such a joy to know.

276

A DAUGHTER'S PRAISE

She says you are nice and pretty
She says you are kind and sweet
She also says you're very generous
The smartest mom that I should meet

If you listen to your children
The truth will soon be known
Children always tell the truth
About what goes on at home

From all the things I've heard
I surely must surmise
You certainly are the greatest mom
In your daughter's eyes

Don't let all that praise
Put your head up in a cloud
You're probably just an average mom
Of whom your daughter's very proud!
06.10.79

Dedicated to Kay Brooks, Lara's mom. The Brooks were our
neighbors when we lived in Irving, Texas. When Laura came over
to visit us, she always bragged on everything her mom and dad
did. A tribute to good parents.

LORA...
An Imaginative Child

Sweet little girl
Imaginative mind
Exciting, enthusiastic
Gentle and kind

Like spring strewing flowers
In magic bouquets
This enchanting child
Frolics and plays

Her warmth and her softness
Her spontaneous ways
Add splashes of sunshine
To brighten my days

Her effervescent spirit
Beyond all compare
She captivates my heart
With her flamboyant flair
04.20.79

Dedicated to Lora Kimberlin Archer Tindall, who is the daughter of
my co-worker and friend, Dr. Richard Tindall. Lora designated me
as her "Grandmother Office." When she came to the office to see
her dad, she always came to visit me, too. Her sisters followed
suit, and I am their Grandmother Office, also. I kind of liked the
title.

HEATHER...
A Tiny spark of Sweetness

A tiny spark of sweetness
Stepped into my room
Just a breath of springtime
Like flowers all in bloom

With the warmest hugs and kisses
And a smile just meant for me
She won my heart entirely
With the love she bestowed on me

Her warm and radiant eyes
And her little pixie smile
In a twinkling of a minute
Made her like my own grandchild

I'll give her lots of love
Like she just gave to me
Her special "Grandmother Office"
I will forever be
06.13.80

Dedicated to Heather Combs Archer Tindall, the middle daughter
of my co-worker and friend, Dr. Richard Tindall. Their own
grandmothers live out of state, so I was adopted as "another
grandmother" by Dr. Tindall's daughters. They designated me as
their "Grandmother Office" to distinguish me from their
grandmother who lives in California whom they call "Grandmother
California."

ASHLEY...
My Little Missing Star

Twinkle, twinkle little star
Grandmother wonders where you are
To your Dad I'll address my plea
Bring Ashley by for me to see

He speaks of you with a proud word
But time's flying by, so it's absurd
For me to miss your sweetest time
When you are young and in your prime

Such a wonderful thing it would be
If your dad brought you by for me to see
I'd hug you, kiss you and love you so
Watch you play and watch you grow

We would be such great friends
Your twinkling eyes and funny grins
Would win my love and touch my heart
We should not have to be apart.

I miss my little twinkling star
You delight me by the way you are
You bring me joy and happiness
Seeing you is what I miss
6.15.80

Dedicated to Ashley Jean Archer Tindall, my co-worker and friend Dr. Richard Tindall's youngest daughter. Ashley also calls me "Grandmother Office," along with her two sisters. Since she is not in school yet, she isn't with her dad as often as her sisters when he picks them up after school and brings them by the office. So, I don't see her very often. She is the star of the show always.

TO MY FRIENDS
SWEETEST DREAMS

We hope every day
The whole year through
Holds everything
You'd like it to

And all your hopes
And sweetest dreams
Be fulfilled for you
By all means

May God bless you
Along your way
Majestic adventures
Await you each day
04.04.04

JONATHAN JAY...
Let's Talk

Hello, sweet little one
How are you today?-
How about a little talk?
I've have lots of things to say

Let's chat about the birds
And discuss gigantic trees
I'll describe the pretty flowers
And explain about the bees

There are lots of things in life
You will need to know
I'll teach it all to you
As you start to grow

You'll want to learn about
Things we call "antique"
And you'll need to know
About the future you will seek
Continued

I'm really looking forward
To all our quiet, long talks
And watching you grow tall
And helping you to walk

The time will come, I'm sure
When I'll have a shocked surprise
As you start to answer me
With astonishing replies

So I can hardly wait
'Til you sit upon my knee
And I can talk to you
And you can **answer** me
07.17.82

Dedicated to Jonathan Jay Pettigrew (1982-2002) He died in a car accident. Jonathan was the son of Drs. Jay and Nancy Pettigrew, UTHSCD, co-workers and friends. I am grieved that we never did have an opportunity to "just talk." They moved away and we lost contact, which is so regrettable.

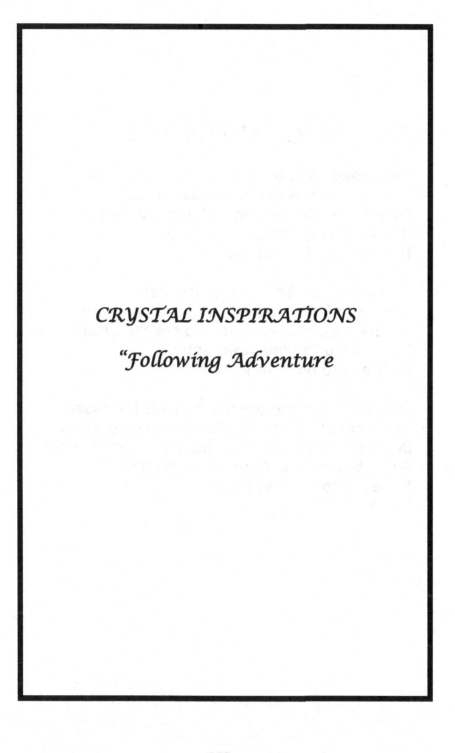

CRYSTAL INSPIRATIONS

"Following Adventure

FOLLOWING....ADVENTURE

The unexpected awaits off the beaten path
Courage ensues daring to take a chance
Adventure intrigues unexplored and remote
Overwhelming curiosity abounds
To see -- to do -- to know

Challenges confront the conqueror
New experiences allure us to the unknown
Adventure beguiles us to explore the future
Conquering the unknown entices
To see -- to do -- to know

Venturing into the unknown defies the blasé
Exploring place to place brings exciting exploits
Down the Snaky River or atop a mountain peak
Going beyond the familiar challenges
To see -- to do -- to know
Continued

Going to remote places...oh, so strange
Discovering untried ground – braving an unknown
Embracing each challenge – scan-search-seek
To see -- to do -- to know

Finding uniqueness face to face with adventure
Following every dream to explore each new place
Never overlooking opportunity for the unique
That was the way of our life
To see -- to do -- to know
03.04.06

Dedicated to my husband, Emery Tuttle who has a most remarkable adventurous spirit to try the new and take me with him. Emery was a WWII pilot but did not renew his pilot's license until he was 76 years old. After which he bought a plane, I decided I could put away all my fears of flying and get my private pilot's license, too. I did, with Emery's encouragement and help. At the age of 67, I became a private pilot and for a while I had my own little Cessna 150. Without Emery in my life, I never would have experienced such an adventure. Thank you, Emery, for helping me to soar to greater things and experience the unknown and conquer my fear and see God's marvelous wonders.

THE HOUSE OF DISREPAIR

Attempting to find the formula
 For wealth's accumulation
We decided first of all to read
 Some books for our edification

Enthused by all the alternatives
 We projected forth our plans
To become self-made millionaires
 We must meet some new demands

We shopped around and finally found
 A house we wanted to buy
It was in a state of disrepair
 A challenge for us to try

You made a list of things to do
 An enormous task to undertake
So intrigued by this great challenge
 Graphic plans you began to make

As you recounted your plans to me
 I had but one suggestion
That we should no longer be the host
 To that termite infestation

You took it lightly and tossed your head
 And mentioned a man who could
Exterminate those little critters
 Before they could eat our wood

So we plunged into the task at hand
 Hammers beating -- sawdust flying
Replacing all worn and broken parts
 Of that run-down house we're buying

Continued

Working with you is such a pleasure
    As you apply all of your energy
There is no challenge we find too great
    For our cooperative synergy

This house looked like a calamity
    With broken windows and rotten wood
It was extremely dilapidated
    But new windows made it look *real* good

Then I started with my commitment
    To tape and bed and paint the walls
It was a task I'd not done before
    But I will "answer" when duty calls

It's amazing what some paint will do
    It will brighten up the dullest room
And give eloquence where once before
    There was nothing there but dirt and gloom

The greatest challenge was yet to come
    It would leave us exasperated
All the utilities needed fixing
    They were extremely antiquated

The pipes all leaked -- the lights didn't work
    So upon your belly you did crawl
Underneath the house you sloshed in mud
    In a space that was much too small

The bathroom floors were a real mess
    Completely rotted through and through
But with your ingenuity and skill
    You made them look brand new

At last the bathroom was complete
    Everything was fixed and in its place
We were proud of our accomplishment
    Apparent by the smile upon your face

Continued

Our friends came to see our accomplishment
We showed them our refurbished bath
We entertained them on our bathroom floor
For hours we sat there to talk and laugh

When our labor was all complete
We couldn't believe our eyes
Our little house of disrepair was
Such an astonishing surprise!
06.02.78

Dedicated to the initiative of Emery Tuttle and the house of disrepair. It was our first house of disrepair that we purchased, fixed up like new, rented, then sold, setting us on our way to hopefully building our wished-for-self-made fortune. We became fast learners and full of new adventure and challenges. We accomplished feats never before tried.

HOUSE
OF
DISREPAIR

REFURBISHED

(WITH POETIC LICENSE)

REMINISCING
The House That He Built

When you first told me that
  By your own hand
You were going to build our house
  It was to my chagrin

All I could visualize was
  It would be a real nightmare
A crooked, leaning shambles
  A real fouled-up-affair

I saw a "self-built house" once
  Just up the road from us
It was a horrendous -- total mess, so
  A "self-built house," I did not trust

In a hundred years -- or so
  Even a thousand or maybe more
I could not have dreamed a "self-built house"
  Would be one I could adore

I didn't realize how talented
  And self-motivated you are
The work you did amazed me
  What wife could ask for more

Everything I wanted done
  You provided it for me
You made it all so beautiful
  And you did it all for me

You fixed a place for everything
  To make my life much easier
You are the sweetest man I know
  A wonderful wife-pleaser
Continued

291

Little nooks and crannies
   Were there for all my things
Lots of shelves for storage
   Even a place for bracelets and rings

"What color do you want?" you'd ask
   I'd reply, "Hot-pink countertops will do"
"O.K," you said, "my dear, I'll get bright
   Hot pink countertops for you!"

Even if it seem redundant
   Like light switches each side of the door
You made it just like I wanted it
   And asked, "Do you need anything more?"

Our friends all said that building a house
   Would assure divorce was on the way
But that didn't ever happen to us
   We loved each other more each day

Building a house together
   Can test you to the limit
But it can also make you stronger
   If you always let God lead it

I married a man who is full
   ...Of vim, vigor and vitality
Living daily with him
   Is an adventure beyond reality

If you find yourself nearby
   Come to see what he did for me
Then you will understand
   How proud this wife can be
01.27.10

Notation and a bit of history:

If you want a real exhilarating adventure, build a house together! There is nothing to compare.

When Emery was 71 years old, he laid out a blueprint for our house, hired a contractor to do what he termed a "dry-in," where the contractor constructed the outside and framed-in the rooms and stairway on the inside, turning it over to us unfinished, without plumbing, electrical, or -- inside walls. We did all the inside work -- carpentry, sheetrock, electrical, plumbing, tape, bedding and painting...all of it by ourselves...we were untrained and slow, but we did it, together!

However, with my husband's unbelievable skill, talent and tenacity, and with my decorating ability, we have a "dream house that suits *our* dream." I have unbelievable custom storage space and conveniences....And the topper is -- it's all paid for. Pay-as-you-build, that was our motto. I love my man. And by the way, we truly actually grew closer together day by day. We are enjoying our retirement on the lake in a paid-for, two-story custom-made-by-us home.

THE ADVENTUROUS SPIRIT

If you have that certain aptitude
For fantastic discoveries
Out of unsuspecting places
You will uncover these

An adventurous spirit
Leads you far and wide
Beckoning you to explore
The world from every side

Your curiosity transports you
To never ceasing wonders
Impromptu adventures intrigue you
While the world around you slumbers

A brightly blazing fire within you
Dances and flickers just once more
Signaling you again to action
Spiraling you as n'er before

Stirring experiences abound
That are often missed by most
Because they refuse to venture
Past the starting post
07.31.85

Dedicated to my husband Emery Tuttle and the memories of all
the astounding adventures he brought into my life. He took me
past the starting post many, many times.

THE MYSTICAL CARIBBEAN

A sleek and graceful ship
Glides across the deep blue seas
The golden moon floats in the sky
Lighting these enchanting Cays

Where islands with romantic names
Offer solace, beauty, charm
Fascinating people living there
Unpretentious, tender, warm

A gentle breeze brushes across the shore
Sweeping aimlessly through the trees
Coconuts falling to the earth
Dislodged by the gentle breeze

There's a lifetime of adventure
Unspoiled and awe-inspiring
With all its primitive beauty
Challenging and inviting

We yearn to travel there again
Engulfed with its serenity
Fond aspirations will linger with us
Throughout all eternity
04.15.78

Dedicated to all our adventures and fond memories we have
shared over the years.

ON THE WAY TO
STANN CREEK TOWN

We saw a man sitting there
Waiting beside the road
He waved his hand; he waved his hand
Sitting by the road to Stann Creek Town

We stopped a minute
He beckoned to us
This is what he said; this is what he said
Waiting beside the road to Stann Creek Town

I beg your pardon, Sir
Would it be possible
To catch a lift; to catch a lift
Going down to Stann Creek Town

Then he said I was hoping
Someone would pass by
Traveling down; traveling down
Traveling down the road to Stann Creek Town

Well I've just been home
For Easter holidays
But must go back; but must go back
Must go back to Stann Creek Town

Thank you kindly, sir, for a lift
Been waiting here since nine
Few pass by; few pass by
Going down to Stann Creek Town
Continued

The journey's long
The weather's warm
I 'preciate; I 'preciate
Getting a lift to Stann Creek Town

There is much to see on the way
Traveling down this road
I'll point it out; I'll point it out
On the way to Stann Creek Town

The miles flew by
There were new things to see
Had so much fun; had so much fun
Going down to Stann Creek Town

We made a good friend
In a country so strange
Because we stopped; because we stopped
On the road to Stann Creek Town

Drove through the hills
Stopped at "Blue-Hole" pool
A sight to see; a sight to see
Along the road to Stann Creek Town

Six miles from town
We encountered his dream
A "Center for Kids"; a "Center for Kids"
Outside the city of Stann Creek Town
Continued

The kids crowded in close
We were strangers to them
They were friendly to us; they were friendly to us
At the Center for Kids near Stann Creek Town

All day they worked hard
Painting the Center for Kids
Back home they'll go; back home they'll go
Back home six miles to Stann Creek Town

They all piled in our car
With their brushes and paint
We took them all home; we took them all home
Six miles back home to Stann Creek Town

The day was not through
There were more things to do
Went out on the town; went out on the town
We danced all night in Stann Creek Town

What started out just to be
A long, lonely drive
Became so exciting; became so exciting
All the way to Stann Creek Town

We recall that day often
When we offered a lift
To a man on the road; to a man on the road
Going down to Stann Creek town
Continued

You'll know what we mean
About the fun that we had
On that wonderful day; on that wonderful day
Traveling the road to Stann Creek Town

If you ever should see him
Waiting beside that road
Give him a lift; give him a lift
On your way to Stann Creek Town

Say hello to him
Ask how he is
If you see that man; if you see that man
Waiting for a lift to Stann Creek Town

Rueben Nunez's his name
In Stann Creek Town he resides
Get to know him; get to know him
If ever you go down to Stann Creek Town
04.06.78

Dedicated to Rueben Nunez, Director of Community Affairs, the
Center for Kids in Stann Creek Town, Belize, Central America, He
made our vacation to Belize memorable and exciting; it was such
a delightful adventure with the man going down to Stann Creek
Town.

PLACENCIA

Placencia was a mess!
It put us to the test
No place to sleep
No place to eat
  Placencia was a mess!

The trip by boat was great
Although we were running late
A nice cool breeze
Crystal-clear blue seas
  The trip by boat was great

Backward was the town
Thatched-roof houses all around
Yards piled high
Garbage to the sky
  Backward was the town
Continued

The people were a clan
Neither woman, child, nor man
No greeting to us was made
To themselves they all stayed
    The people were a clan

The ocean was such a delight
Sparkling with bright sunlight
Waves kissed the beach
Seashells lay within reach
    The ocean was a delight

Placencia was a fright!
How sick I was that night
I felt so bad with what I had
Leaving really, really make me glad
    Placencia was a fright!
04.06.78

Dedicated to our vacation in Placencia, Belize, Central
America -- a dismal place to visit, but interesting nonetheless.

BELIZE BY THE SEA

Gentle sea breeze
Blowing through my hair
I can't really see you
But I know you're there

Tiny, tiny seashells
Resting on the sand
Never have been touched
By the hand of man

Living, crawling creatures
Residing in the ocean
Darting to and fro again
As you take a notion

Sparkling, glistening sunlight
Splashing on the sea
Moonlight's soft warmth glowing
With its beckoning plea
Continued

See black-coral divers
Taking all those chances
Bringing up their treasure
Causing envious glances

Snorkelers with their goggles
Watching all the fish
Sliding through the waters
With such cunningness

Boats of all descriptions
Gliding across the sea
Sailing where their masters
Think they want to be

Belize, the tiny country
We ventured down to see
What I liked the best was
Belize nestled by the sea
04.06.78

Dedicated to our adventurous, exciting vacation in Belize, Central
America at San Pradre Ambergris Caye, Belize.

le Baton Rouge
"RED POLE ON THE BLUFF"

A beautiful spring day
Magnolias all in bloom
Away from bustling crowds
And hazy, smoke-filled rooms

Le Baton Rouge --
Where history has been made
By men filled with vision
With hearts unafraid

A lively, modern city
A pleasant atmosphere
Beckoned me to visit
To share the history there

Upon the lawn was a replica
Of the much-honored *Liberty Bell*
Its weighty clapper I noted
And admired with some detail

Simple, romantic beauty
With its stately charm
If I were to gently *push it*
Surely would do no harm
Continued

Then a *wild* crescendo roared
Through beautiful, landscaped grounds
I looked for an *invisible* spot
To hide me from its sound

Expecting whirling guards
My pulsating heart grew weak
I left the grounds abruptly
Adventure elsewhere to seek

The look upon your face
Reflected what you would say
Like..."I don't know that girl
Who rang that bell today!"

Experiencing a lively mixture
Of excitement and curiosity
I knew a spectacular departure
Was in order with extreme velocity

Clamoring that great *Liberty bell*
Had its own little frenzy in it
But deep-down inside, I must confess
I loved every, single minute
06.13.79

Dedicated to our day in Baton Rouge, Louisiana, where Emery
wouldn't admit he even knew me. An unplanned, loud...very
loud...adventure.

LADY OF THE STAGE

Lady of the stage
With your boisterous ways
Never did you please me
In the olden days

I did not admire you
In that boisterous style
Tonight you amused me
After all this while

I cannot explain why
You captivated me this time
With all those little tea bags
Hanging neatly on the line

What made that so funny
Why did I laugh so
At all your little tea bags
Hanging in a row

Your style is still quite marked
By a manner coarse and rowdy
And you were all decked out
In costumes grossly dowdy
Continued

Your exuberance and high spirits
Warmed me to the core
And your dazzling performance
Kept me rolling on the floor

I had come prepared
To be bored almost to tears
Instead I laughed much more
Than I had laughed in years

Lady of the stage
Tonight my heart you've won
You intrigued and fascinated me
By your performance so well done
08.31.78

Dedicated to Martha Raye's performance in "Everybody Loves Opal," at Granny's Dinner Theatre, Dallas, Texas; a funny adventure. That night I learned to appreciate what I had over looked before...talent.

REMEMBER THE DAY

Remember the day
When we went out to play
With horses and ducks and geese?
    We saw sheep without fleece
    Then a goat walked high on a rail

The water was blue
There were bicycles for two
The grass was as green as a pea
    Over our head flew a bee
    And the donkey was wagging his tail

We ate junk food for our lunch
Oh what a great bunch
Of fun we had on that day
    We thought we forever should stay
    But the ants ate the bread that was stale

Remember the day
When we went out to play
What a wonderful fun time we had
    The experiences made our hearts glad
    'Til the soft wind turned into a gale
09.01.03

Dedicated to a play-day of adventure on a picnic. Adventure is everywhere. All you have to do is look around you and you will find adventure in a place, a person, a thing, an event and in every part of God's nature from the deepest cave to the highest mountain and everything in between...Just look for it, and enjoy.

THE HEALTH KICK!

Joggers in the morning
  In their jogging suit
Running off the pounds
  As if in pursuit

Fishing paraphernalia
  For the fishermen
Every pound of fish that's caught
  Will cost him six to ten

Over there's the hunter
  Waiting for his prey
If he doesn't get one
  He'll come back another day

Oops! There goes the golfer
  Going off the tee
Aiming for the hole
  But he hits a tree

But what is done most often
  To get our exercise
Is just to **watch** a ballgame
  And exercise our eyes!
04.15.85

Dedicated to our adventures by experience. Jogging -- been there, done that...didn't like it then, don't like it now! My outlook is based upon our experience jogging to get ready for our hike to the bottom of the Grand Canyon where we set up our camp site. I like "watching" exercises a lot better than "doing" exercises. Now that I am older...I exercise my eyes a lot more!

COWBOY FANS

Cheer if you will -- sneer if you will
From the crowd let loud noises ring
Wave your kerchief high in the air
When the victory song you sing

Cheer if you will -- sneer if you will
But if the opponent happens to score
Thumb a scarf from the end of your nose
And stomp your feet on the floor

Cheer if you will -- sneer if you will
All true Cowboy fans are known
By the wave of their kerchiefs high in the air
When they're singing their victory song
11.07.72

Dedicated to just "watching" adventure happen. Yeah, Cowboys--
Go, Cowboys, Go! I'm a real true Texas Cowgirl...Cowboy fan.

CRYSTAL INSPIRATIONS

"Reasons For Celebrating

IT'S JUST A BIRTHDAY
Don't Look So Sad

Don't look so sad
It's just a birthday
Getting older is not
Really so dreadfully bad

Don't look so sad
Birthdays come just once a year
You're getting a little older
That's not particularly bad

Don't look so sad
It won't help one little bit
To dread a birthday 'cause
You'll see it's not all that bad

Don't look so sad
Ask your friends who know
Getting older actually is better
Than *the* alternative – that's *bad!*
04.26.09

Dedicated to any reason to celebrate -- birthdays being special.
They come regularly and often and are for everyone. So let's
celebrate!

YOU SAY...
You're Not Getting Older!

You say you're not getting *older*
But only getting a lot *better*
That grandson sitting on your knee
Fits *older* to-the-letter!

You say your walk is just *high steppin'*
And the *shufflin's* just an act
But we all know your walk is caused
By *arthritis* in your back

The painted eyes, the glued-on nails
Really are just a cover up
This is the *truth* -- you're an *AARPie girl*
And not a *frisky* pup

We know your age by the way you talk
About your aches and pains
For that's the way all *AARPies* talk
You all sound just the same

The days have come; the days have gone
And this one thing is true
You really are just *getting old*
For you sure ain't *getting new!*
04.03.91

Dedicated to Winnie Walton, UTHSCD, co-worker, friend, and to my little *AARPie girl* I say--Happy Birthday. True, you may be *older* but you really do still *look young.*

HAPPY, HAPPY BIRTHDAY
To A Very Young Girl

To a very young girl
Who has lived a long time
I send "Birthday Wishes"
With verses and rhyme

I'll tell you something
This girl has learned
It will help you through
The birthdays you've spurned

Birthdays will come and
Birthdays will go
But that doesn't mean
Your age has to show

Smile when your birthday
Rolls past again
Don't even whisper
How many it's been

Your friends won't remember
How old you have gotten
If they should ask you
Just say you've forgotten

You're still cute as a bug
And charmin' as well
I hope that this birthday
Turns out really swell
11.24.02

MATTHEW 6:25, 27

"...do not be anxious for your life,
As to what you shall eat,
or what you shall drink;
nor for your body,
as to what you shall put on...
And which of you by being anxious
can add a single cubit
to his life's span?..."

WE ALL GET OLDER EVERY DAY

The year has come -- and gone so fast
Your birthday's here again -- at last!

You said that you were getting *slimmer*
All I've noticed is your eyes grow *dimmer*

Your hair's a bit *lighter* is your claim
But *gray's* really that color's name

Your walk is *slower* -- your shoulders *bent*
It looks to me like this year was *spent*

What can we do -- what more to say
We all get *older* every day!

HAPPY BIRTHDAY ONE MORE OLDER TIME
03.03.91

Dedicated to Dimitri Proctor Anderson, UTHSCD, co-worker and friend who looks "*younger*" even when she's getting "*older*."

TO CELEBRATE THE DAY
Of Your Birth

I love to celebrate the birth
Of one I love so dearly
And hope these humble words
Express my love sincerely

You are my dearest friend
And I wanted you to know
The passing of another year
Marks how much my love did grow

With the passing of the years
We may grow old and get some wrinkles
But the love of friends stays bright and strong
Like a star that brightly twinkles

Happy Birthday, dearest friend
More love to you this year than last
More hope and joy and peace and grace
And all God's precious gifts that last
C E L E B R A T E
01.01.01

REMEMBER
Means Don't forget

Wrinkles -- are just your laugh lines
Forgetting -- is conservation of your brain power
Overweight -- is a way to store your energy
Getting older -- is just maturing like fine wine

So...

Grab a bottle of wine and enjoy forgetting that
You are getting older, *fatter, forgetful* and
Full of...What was that? Oh yeah -- laugh wrinkles

HAVE A HAPPY BIRTHDAY
LAUGH...ANYWAY
07.18.08

TO THE OLD YEAR
We Best Bid Adieu

You were fresh, alive
  Enthusiastic, strong
Promising happiness
  Sunshine and song

We romped and we frolicked
  Shed tears; had some strife
We took things in stride
  As all part of life

But now the moments
  Tick quietly away
Let's reminisce
  In our special way

Let's run back through
  The pathway of time
Recall all the moments
  Which were so sublime

I had my full share
  Of happiness with you
But the end now approaches
  We best bid adieu

As part of my heritage
  You'll n'er disappear
But I must bid you adieu
  As I greet a New Year
12.31.80

Dedicated to every Happy New Year, because each new year
gives us a reason to celebrate and a new opportunity and a clean
page to do it better Say adieu to the old and hello to the new.

THE NEW YEAR
The Land Of Beginning Again

Oh where is that land --
That land of beginning again?
We long to set forth on the voyage
To find that land

Leaving all past mistakes behind
Reviving our sinking hearts
Finding peace and contentment
Like ne'er before we've known

Oh where is that land --
Where happiness surely lurks?
Every age has its problems
Every heart has its sorrows

We search endlessly for happiness
Yet we exhaust it by consuming it
We find thousands of momentary delights
But they are all fleeting -- inadequate

Oh where is that land of beginning again?
Too often we lose courage in the search
We must not be disheartened though
Because there is a land of beginning again

Beginning again we enter each time anew
Reaching for better things
Oh where is that land of beginning again?
It lies within the heart
01.01.82

ANOTHER CHANCE
To Get It Right

A New Year is in your hands
  Like a book with unspotted pages
Fresh, for nothing yet is recorded there
  But as soon as you receive it
It becomes like a ticking clock
  Counting off the minutes; it begins
Recording both good and bad
  A New Year is in your hands
If you do not use wisely
  It will become like an old, frayed book
Useless...without value
  God holds each New Year in trust for you
Protected by His hand
  He will guide you, lead you every day
If you let Him take command
  A New Year is in your hands
Allow God to take control
  He'll give you peace like calm, quiet rivers
And wash all your cares away
  He'll speak quietly like a tranquil breeze
On a long, warm summer's day
  You have another chance to learn
From all that's gone before
  A New Year is in your hands
Thus only you can turn the page
  Whatever you write on each page
Will be determined by your choices
  God has given you a New Year
Make each day count and when it's through
  You can look back and count its value
01.01.84

SOON A NEW YEAR

The days are whizzing by
Weeks fly into months
One season blends into another
A year has passed again

It's heartwarming to look back
Viewing happenings that transpired
Were the days filled with laughter
Or were they just monotonous?

With an assortment of projects
And numerous places to go
We shared traditions and sentiments
With friends both new and old

While we round up our thoughts
To refresh our memories
We recalled the promises made
And reviewed our New Year's vows

We are counting down the minutes
Until the old year has completely past
When we can have a fresh start
To begin from the top again
12.31.06

START OVER

When you've trusted God and walked His way
When you've felt His hand lead you day by day
When you have faltered then taken another way
---Start over

When you've made plans and they've gone awry
When you've tried your best and can no longer try
When you've failed yourself and you don't know why
---Start over

When you've told your friends what you plan to do
When you've trusted them -- they don't come through
When you're all alone and it's only you
---Start over

When you've prayed to God so you can know His will
When you've prayed and prayed but don't know still
When you want to stop because you've had your fill
---Start over
Continued

322

When you think you're finished and you want to quit
When you've bottomed out in life's deepest pit
When you've tried and tried to get out of it
---Start over

When you've failed your kids and now they're gone
When you've done your best but it turned out wrong
When grandchildren now have come along
---Start over

When the year's been long and successes few
When December comes and you're feeling blue
Remember God provided January first for you
---To start over

When starting over means -- "Victories can be Won"
When starting over means -- "A Race Well Run"
When starting over means -- "God's Will Is Done"
---Don't sit there, just...START OVER
01.01.01

SPECIAL MOMENT

There are special moments
---To start again afresh
---To share with one another
---To remember forgotten dreams
Lost in life's busy streams

We have those special moments
---To experience uncluttered love
---To see the smallest leaf
---To hear the sweetest sounds
Lost as our daily life abounds

Let's take this special moment
---To be completely unafraid
---To give all the love we can
---To rediscover a long lost joy
Lost moments can be enjoyed

01.02.81

AGAPE LOVE FOR A
HAPPY VALENTINE's DAY

May the Lord bless and fill you with His agape love
As He watches over you from Heaven above
He allows us to be His hands and His feet
To touch one another with His love so sweet

Agape love is love like no other love can be
God sent His love through Christ to you and me
God's agape love is a love divine
I give to you my agape love, dear Valentine
02.14.94

Dedicated to everyone in love. Valentine is the sweetest time to celebrate love and the best kind of love to give is God's agape love...which is a freely given gift...unconditional love...unmerited love.

THE EASTER EGG HUNT

Scurrying children
Scampering to and fro
Diligently searching
Every cranny high and low

Bright-colored eggs
Patiently abide
In secret places
Until suddenly they're spied

With wide-eyed innocence
The children are so cute
As successfully and triumphantly
They gathered up their loot
04.15.75

LIFE'S MOMENTS

Life's moments should be
A series of joyous
Live-to-the-fullest
Unexpected moments

Always keeping me
Serene and confident
Triumphantly vital
Enhancing my very being
09.28.72

HAPPY EASTER

April is the time all the children know
The Easter bunny visits us
To leave happy eggs to show

We celebrate a happy Easter season
Because Jesus' love paid the price for us
Consequently we rejoice for that very reason

We forever remember the purpose why
Jesus had to died upon the cross was
That none of us should die

They nailed his hands and pierced his side
When they hung him from that cross so
To pay our debt upon that cross...He died

Although Christ died to pay the price
God raised Him from the dead!
Our debt was paid by Christ's own sacrifice

To God our Father we sing alleluias and praise
Because He sent His only Son to die for us
For unmerited love we will thank Him always
04.10.07

JOHN 11:25-26

"I am the resurrection and the life;
he who believes in Me
Shall live even if he dies,
and everyone who lives
and believes in Me shall never die
Do you believe this?..."

A MYSTICAL NIGHT

Did you know soon it will be the night
Goblins come out for the kiddies' delight
With spooks and ghosts and witches galore
All the mystical things the kiddies adore

Games and pranks, with trick-or-treating
Popcorn balls and sweet candy eating
Frightened by the superstitious spells
And scary stories that grandfather tells

Of howling winds and full, bright moons
Being face-to-face with dreaded goons
Then running away, filled with dread fright
And meeting a witch-on-a-broomstick in flight

An eerie night, a shrieking sound
A haunted house with spooks all around
Hair-raising adventures awaiting there
Being filled with terror and chilling fear

This hairy, scary, exciting night
Is a mixture of both ghastly fear and delight
At the stroke of twelve all spooks disappear
Then all is quiet until the next year
10.31.73

HALLOWEEN

'Tis the night of witches and goblins
With skeletons and ghosts on parade
It's also the time when vampires come out
And really weird noises are made

If you should see a huge, black cat
Look quickly up in the sky
The silhouette you see on the moon
Is just a witch passing by

A big, old house all filled with ghosts
Will scare all the kids on the street
Inside you can hear rattling chains
And some bats you'll probably meet

The air is filled with excitement
The children scurry and flee
Every time they hear a noise
Every time a goblin they see

But Halloween is so intriguing
House-to-house they eagerly go
Looking for lots of tricks and treats
And a bewitching ghost to show
10.31.73

Happy Halloween to my granddaughters, Amy and Alicia.
I remember the days when I took your daddy trick-or-treating.

GOBLINS

Tap, tap, tap – Tap, tap, tap
Something's knocking on my door
Tap, tap, tap -- Tap, tap, tap
I heard it knock again once more

Adventure beckoned to me
From the chilling night
The mystic moon was shinning
But I was filled with fright

Who is lurking outside my door
I see a glimpse of him
But I can't see a face too clearly
'Cause the light outside's so dim

Tap, tap, tap -- Tap, tap, tap
I heard that knock again
Maybe it will go away
I'm afraid to let it in

I hear weird moans and groans
Now there's a flickering light
It excites my keenest senses
To hear strange sounds at night

I know there are spooks and goblins
Traveling everywhere tonight
They'll bewitch you with their magic
So everyone be quiet

Tap, tap, tap -- Tap, tap, tap
There it goes again
Please don't open up the door
Don't let the goblins in

Outside the moon's still shining
And the noise I hear is shrilling
I have an unforgettable fear
Nonetheless the sound is thrilling

Tap, tap, tap -- Tap, tap, tap
This intruder I must greet
Then just as I opened up the door
The goblins yelled, "Trick or Treat!"
10.27.73

P.S. To set the record straight, I don't believe in ghosts and
goblins. However, I grew up with Trick-or-Treating at Halloween
and it is hard to discord old habits and events that were happy
times in childhood.

PSALM 27:1

"...The Lord is my light and my salvation;
Whom shall I fear?
The Lord is the defense of my life;
Whom shall I dread?..."

THANKSGIVING DAY
Is On The Way

Thanksgiving Day is on the way
It's time for us to stop and pray
To thank our God in Heaven above
For blessing us with all His love

Sincerely, dear Lord, we do thank you
We're grateful, God, for all you do
For family and friends, both old
and new
We ask you, Lord, to bless them, too

11.25.08

LUKE 2:10-11

"...Do not be afraid; for behold,
I bring you good news of a great
joy which shall be for all the people;
for today in the City of David there
has been born for you a Savior,
who is Christ the Lord..."

DO YOU KNOW THE REASON
For The Christmas Season?

Do you wait for Santa
And the gifts that he might bring?
Or does the thought of Jesus' birth
Start your heart to sing?

If it's just a gift you want
I have the very best
It's what God has done for you
For me and for all the rest

He gave His only Son
To rescue us from sin
And if you will believe in Him
He'll keep you to the end

Ask Jesus into your heart today then
You will understand the reason
God sent His only Son to be
Your gift this Christmas season
09.09.09

Dedicated to the precious gift that God gave to mankind...His only
begotten Son who died for us that we might have eternal life.

CHRISTMAS GREETINGS

Winter, spring, summer, fall
Christmas greetings to you all
Seems we've passed another year
Again it's time to send our cheer

When I retired I thought my time
Would be so free and be all mine
But I have found that's not the case
Retirement just increased my pace

Though I only sing and play all day
Nonetheless, time slips away
Oh it would never, ever do
To fail to send our cheer to you

So "Christmas Greetings" once again
I send to you our special friend
Our prayer's that God will send you cheer
By blessing you through all next year!
12.01.95

1 JOHN 4:14-15

"...And we have beheld and bear witness
That the Father has sent the Son
To be the Savior of the world
Whosoever confesses that
Jesus is the Son of God
God abides in im
And He in God..."

MERRY CHRISTMAS
HAPPY HANUKKAH

Shimmering, glittering gold and silver
A wealth of wreaths and garlands
Dazzling trees glowing with lights
Making beautiful holiday wonderlands

Tender moments you won't forget
Smiling faces and loving hearts
Enveloped in a spirit of love
This magical season starts

Holiday greetings from far-away friends
Fill your heart with endearing gladness
The season brings a lot of joy
And a little of touch of sadness

Anticipation will fill the air with
Each package placed under the tree
Everyone plays guessing games
"What's in that package for me?"

Preparations are being made
For a truly scrumptious dinner
Everyone will leave the table
Much happier...but not much thinner

If indeed this holiday season
Should bring you happiness
Please pass it on to others
With a "Happy Holiday" kiss
11.30.79

Notation: To my UTHSCD Christian and Jewish friends and co-workers. Put a little mistletoe on the door; it will tie the two of you together. Don't miss that kiss, just kiss your miss, it's good in any weather.

NUMBERS 6:24-26

"...The Lord bless you, and keep you
The Lord make His face shine on you
And be gracious to you;
The Lord lift up His countenance on
you,
And give you peace..."

I WILL BLESS THE LORD

I will bless the Lord
And give Him glory
I will bless His name
And give Him glory

I will bless You Lord
And give You glory
I will bless Your name
And give You glory

You are the Great I Am
I bless you, Lord
I will give you glory
You are the great I Am
08.19.10

THERE'S GONNA BE LOTS OF TIME
(Song)

There's gonna be time to talk in Heaven
   To tell the story of God's love
There's gonna be time to talk in Heaven
   To tell Jesus of our love

There's gonna be time to share in Heaven
   About the miracles of God's love
There's gonna be time to share in Heaven
   All the things Christ did in love

There's gonna be time to talk in Heaven
   And lots of time for sharing
There's gonna be lots of time in Heaven
   For us to share God's love

Refrain:

Yes there's gonna be time
   (echo) There's gonna be time

There's gonna be lots of time
   Up above
   (echo) Up above

There's gonna be time in Heaven
To tell the story of God's love
   (echo) the story of God's love
06.27.83

CRYSTAL INSPIRATIONS

"Observing God's' Creation
At Work"

THE EMERGENCE OF SPRING

We welcome the emergence of spring
The season of new beginnings
Inspiring us to be energized
Ready to take on the world

We began kicking off our shoes
And rolling up our sleeves to get ready
To take on the tasks nature requires
To plant a tree...to reap a harvest

Its time to support our favorite team
Displaying their skills, making us proud
The green grass invites brisk walks and
Lazy days of siestas in swinging hammocks

Spring's exciting adventures await us
Bidding us to venture into the unknown
We no longer daydream about these escapades
The outdoors offers to the inquisitive explorer
Continued

The birds commence their love songs
Butterflies scurry flower to flower
Nature provides amazing insight and acuity
As it struggles to break forth new life

How satisfying it is to delight in its rejuvenation
Spring air is filled with crisp, vibrant fragrances
The soothing richness of the aroma lends itself
To a healing restoration of body and spirit

The winter-weary adventurer is refreshed
Anticipating an invigorating connection to nature
Flashing back to indelible memories of inspiration
Stimulated by the extraordinary marvels of spring

Nature provides a palette of color for the artist
A poem for the poet and a story for the author
Nature offers every artist opportunity to elaborate
On the emergence of spring's rich offerings
02.17.10

THE ECSTASIES OF SPRING

Spring issues a flush of feelings
Because every living thing around me
Has beauty and excitement and
The world is full of its ecstasy

Spring comes strewing flowers
With romantic mystery
To the winter-weary flower lovers
Spring brings spectacular ecstasy

Spring provides incredible sounds
The melodious birds in trees
Arouse in the human heart
Unforgettable ecstasies

Spring scatters lazy clouds through the sky
In the trees with its gentle breeze
Blissfully spring rocks the boroughs
In a peaceful ecstasy

Spring anoints the world with magic
Granting every wish and plea
The earth bursts forth with a taste of life
Spreading eternal ecstasy
04.27.99

THE JOY OF SPRING

The joy of spring reminds us
   That we have a living Lord
It symbolizes eternal life
   As promised in His Word

The beauty of spring flowers
   Should set our hearts at ease
For Solomon in all his splendor
   Was not arrayed as these

Every living creature
   Has God's special love and care
Even when a sparrow falls
   God is surely there

We have bouquets of flowers
   To remind us of God above
And all the promises He's given us
   Of His eternal love
04.04.83

Notation: Spring is our symbol of eternal life and the resurrection.

SPRING IS IN THE AIR

Shimmering dewdrops pierce the sleeping earth
in the midst of an awakening spring
Lazy clouds roll by; vivid whiteness is pressed against
a deep blue sky, constantly changing the appearance

The promise of spring penetrates the air
miracles are expressed in spring's rich abundance
We share in spring's unfolding dramas when gardens
...flaunt their multi-colors against the azure sky

Our excitement rises as we can take increasing delight
...in the vibrant splendor of God's miracle of life
We feel a quickening, an excitement at the sound
...of melodious birds in flight soaring through the sky

The promise of spring stirs every emotion, excites our
...keenest senses to anticipate what the future holds
Grass shinning like millions of diamonds in the sunlight
...anointed with morning dew falling from the quiet sky

Flowers decorate the countryside with startling beauty
...exhibiting exquisite colors -- provocative fragrances
We linger for a moment for a romantic rendezvous
...every emotion stirred by what God has created

Small private longings arise as we are observing
...the glory of nature captured in cheery rich colors
Harmonious sounds from earth and sky intrigue us
...and fill us with ecstatic awe and wonderment

Spring with an unhurried dignity and stateliness of age
...is also as impetuous and spontaneous as youth
Spring makes a fresh impact upon every generation
...vindicating and asserting itself as miraculous

You can't remain a skeptic, a cynic, nor, a non-believer
...not in the midst of a miraculous, exotic spring
Spring turns our head toward God's handiwork
...and kindles our belief in our Eternal Almighty God
03.01.99

A SUDDEN SPRING STORM

Clouds spread relentlessly
Across the brewing sky so grand
Weaving a tapestry of energy
To wage fury upon the land

Frightening and beautiful
Awesome and foreboding
As suddenly as it appeared, it
Abruptly dissipates without warning

The evaporating moisture tempered
With the heavy aroma of rain
Lingers as a bleak reminder
A storm can not be tamed

The sunlight emerges softly
Until the sky glows bright once more
But that does not suggest at all
A storm will not again o'er this land roar
03.29.99

SPRING FEVER
There Must Be A Better Way

Sulfur and molasses in the spring
Was in the past traditional
Although it tasted awful
They said it was nutritional

There **must** be a better way to
Produce spring's "rejuvenated-sense"(sic)
And turn a winter-weary body
Into a youthful effervescence!
04.27.99

SAVE SOME SUMMER FOR WINTER

Our lives are sweetened and enriched
  By the fragrance and beauty of the earth
As newborn leaves sprout forth
  And flowers unfold delicate petals
We are rendered speechless at their beauty
  And stand in awe in their majestic presence

Trees stretch forth loving arms
  And gather in the gentle breeze
Rocking to and fro in love's embrace
  Shimmering dewdrops pierce the sleeping earth
The green grass anointed with the morning dew
  Sparkles like millions of diamonds in the sun

Serene and unrestrained we are absorbed
  By the stillness and warmth of the season
Expanding ripples of the waves mesmerize us
  Making silvery creases in tranquil ponds
In a dreaminess occasioned by nature's splendor
  We become alive with exciting things

Cannot summer be for an eternity?
  Per chance, if only it could forever last
Yet nothing is given without a disadvantage
  How sad to see summer end
And the dread of winter overtake us; however
  In our heart we can save some summer for
                ...winter

08.31.99

Notation: Summer is the symbol of God's care and warm love for
all of his creation.

346

LINGERING

Summer stayed late this year
With long days, warm and lazy
The calendar indicates fall is here
But dapper days deny it

Basking in nature's sunlight hours
Trees soak up the prolonged warmth
Fragrances rise from lingering flowers
Intoxicating everyone

With enticing hues of red
The evening sun paints the heavens
In preparation for earth's bed
As twilight enters

Summer must now depart
As it is with all nature's children
One must end to bring the start
Of another's mysterious beginning
10.07.78

THE LEAVES ARE FALLING

The leaves are falling
The wind is blowing
But your birthday cannot come
Without your knowing
We wish the best for all of those
Whose birthdays occur
in the Fall

HAPPY **AUTUMN** BIRTHDAY
10.04.04

Notation: Birthday cards were sent to each of the members of the Cedar Creek Lake Literary Club in the month of their birthday when I was president. Birthdays are the best reason for celebration.

FROST-FREE FUN

Snuggle up to the fireplace
To chase away the winter's chill
Enjoy the magic of the snow
Glistening atop the hill

Suddenly the chill of winter
Takes on a new allure
Children fashion snowmen
Winter blues to cure

But a snazzy snowman
Standing brave and tall
Needs a winter blizzard
So he doesn't melt and fall

But piles of cozy blankets
And cuddling beside the fire
With some frost-free fun inside
Will fulfill all that I desire
02.26.99

THE FALL OF LIFE TURNS TO
WINTER

When the fall of life concludes
We're not yet ready for desuetude
Yet seemingly inevitable succession of events
Determine we must change our attitude

When the winter season touches the earth
The land is left desolate and sterile
We feel like wintertime -- forsaken and abandoned
Aimlessly passing each event in dread of peril

At a time when all outward beauty is fading
Ironically the inward beauty emerges
A special mellowness that only time can give
Quietly, yet tenaciously, within us surges

The youth in us refuses to yield, yet we feel
Vulnerable and unable to defend ourselves
As all our dreams and aspirations
Collect together from the dusty shelves

All we ever wanted to do -- or be
Now influences our melancholy
So we reach out in desperate attempts
To experience one last folly

Then we remember where we're going
And we exclaim, "There's no more hurry"
A sense of security is excited within us
Which softens, then vanishes the needless worry
Continue

What before has been a part of our life
Remains to comfort our loneliness
But new values now emerge
Which fathom all the phoniness

It takes the full cycle of life to gain
Faith, hope, wisdom and perception
Somewhere along the way we change
By accident or deliberate conception

We gain a new quality of life
That which was important long ago
No longer torments our soul
Our life is made richer as we grow old

Contemplating the reality of winter's coming
Awakens us from our dozing
But it's the essence of our inner being
That enables us to no longer fear life's closing
08.31.94

Notation: This was the last day before I retired. Retirement thrusts
us into the winter of our life, but not without hope and the promise
of the forthcoming beauty awaiting us in all of life's seasons. Fall
comes as a notification that life is coming to an end, but we are
given an opportunity to prepare for eternal things. Just as the
farmer prepares the earth in the fall for the emergence of spring,
We must prepare our life for our future eternity. Aging brings a
new sense of deliberation of the issues of real importance in our
life. We are given opportunity as life closes for reconciliation and
restitution.

WINTER'S LOVE
Written in the Snow

God's love spoke gently to me
Disguised in glistening snow
His hand reached out to hold mine
Against a barren winter's tow

Snowflakes fell as coverlets
Over the earth with care
God's love flooded over me with
Tenderness beyond compare

Quietness filled the air
Sunlight pointed out the way
To the love God had for me
On that bleak, cold winter's day

God's ultimate plan He envisioned
When He created each soft snowflake
Each uniquely designed so --
One from another you can't mistake

Continued

I was fascinated and intrigued
To find God's love within the cold
For His love is warm and kind
That's what I was always told

I was elated and overwhelmed
God would reveal to me His majesty
In the serene beauty of the snow
He poured out warm love to me

Warming sunlight broke the crystals
Clarity illuminated my heart
God, who revealed Himself to me today
Had always loved me from the start

In the dread of frigid winter
When the frosty breezes blow
I'll remember a winter's day when
God's eternal love was written in the snow
11.06.99

Notation: Winter is the symbol of life's ending; but, God has chosen to have the evidence of His love and eternal resurrection shown by winter's respite's ending and the emergence of spring with the resurrection of new life.

WINTER'S BUTTERFLY

The snowflake is winter's butterfly
   Flitting to and fro
Spreading the joy of Christmas
   Everywhere it goes

Lighting upon the housetops
   Coverings every blade of grass
Gathering upon the treetops
   Spreading blankets on the paths

If you try to catch a snowflake
   It disappears quickly in your hand
But it has a Christmas magic
   That only children understand

Laughing, running, frolicking then
   Lying in deep piles of snow
Making Christmas angels
   And snowballs they can throw

Like the flitting of the butterfly
   Snowflakes come fluttering down
Giving the earth a beautiful
   White blanket-covered ground
01.25.10

OUR NOSES ARE COLD

Our noses are cold
And our hands are blue
But warm Birthday wishes
We are sending to you

Our hands stay warm
Inside our glove
And our Birthday wishes
Are wrapped in warm love

WARMEST WISHES TO YOU
FOR YOUR WINTERTIME
HAPPY BIRTHDAY
12.04.04

THE SPIRIT OF CHRISTMAS

May the spirit of Christmas
Bring you *Peace*
May the gladness of Christmas
Give you *Hope*
May the warmth of Christmas
Grant you *Love*
May your entire Christmas season
Fill you with *Fun*...and *Friends*
07.18.08

ADIEU, FAREWELL, WINTER!

Farewell winter! It's needless to say
I know you will come back another day
You were lovely with crisp, moon-lit nights
The star-bright skies brought us such delight

You were beckoning weary travelers to seek
Warm, cozy fires your winter's cold to beat
But now it's time for you to say adieu
Behind fluffy clouds the sun is peeking through

Bidding the emergence of cheery birds that sing
Colorful blooms burst forth to create a vivid spring
New seasons follow winter -- spring, summer, fall
Different seasons with a special harmony for all

Spring has glorious flowers, sprinkled with dew
Summer brings ripen berries and sunshine, too
Fall has cascading leaves with vibrant hues
Bringing us cheerful joy until winter comes anew

With snow blankets, winter puts the earth to sleep
Initiating a never-ending cycle the seasons keep
Farewell for now, dear winter! It's needless to say
Each season wears a diverse look in its varied way

Each brings our lives different moods and ecstasy
The splendor displayed amazes and dazzles me
Winter's here today-gone tomorrow; that's its way
But soon winter will come back another day
02.20.99

THE DESERT'S LURE

The desert's warmth beckons those
Who seek respite from the icy-cold
Peace and tranquility quietly wait
Offering an oasis within a lonely vastness
The blossoming cactus puts out welcoming arms
Bidding sun lovers...come, come, come

Brisk, starry nights blanket the earth
After she is put to bed by multi-colored sunsets
She waits the quickening of the dawn
Which touches the horizon with beguiling majesty
Inevitably the sun ascends through the heavens
Enveloping the earth with all its splendor

Who can resist such majestic loveliness
If we should dare return to winter's icy torment
Would we regain our equanimity, that which was
Reverberated by the desert's lure; or, would we
Willingly to succumb to the desert's enticing arms
Returning again to her warmth and charm
who knows?
07.07.99

MATTHEW 16:2-3

*"...When it is evening, you say,
'It will be fair weather, for the sky
is red.'... And in the morning,
'There will be a storm today, for
the sky is red and threatening'..."*

A ROARING THUNDERSTORM

Rafts of clouds crowded together
Billowing, reaching high into an endless sky
Brewing over the rugged earth
With rising energy soaring high

Relentlessly, gathering in chaotic motion
With wild winds swirling with dispassionate force
Moisture gathering, rising to colder heights
Forming ice crystals, spattering noisily, of course

Over terrains thunder roars with stuttering groans
While the winds howl throughout the lofty trees
Powerful and foreboding with awesome fascination
Then as suddenly as it appeared -- it leaves

The land shudders, the sky softens gradually
A glistening mist hovers over the rain-kissed hay
A multi-colored rainbow appears on the horizon
Promising the emergence of another bright day
04.22.99

A MIGHTY STORM WAS BREWING

A mighty storm was brewing
　　Blowing with such forceful power
Nothing was left standing
　　Except one sad and lonely tower

Houses all around
　　Were torn into little pieces
No mercy does the wind show
　　When its mighty force increases

All around homes lay in shambles
　　Lives torn apart, drenched in tears
Everything was gone that families
　　Had collected through the years

What would the future hold for them?
　　How could they start anew?
The sadness overwhelmed them
　　But this one thing is true

God always provides us strength
　　If we let go and rely on Him
Through everything -- thick or thin
　　We must always depend on Him

Mighty storms will come and go
　　Leaving destruction in their path
God always helps us overcome
　　The storms' unyielding wrath
05.05.10

MARK 4:41
*"...Who then is this, that even the
wind and the sea obey Him?"...*

AFTER THE STORM

AFTER THE STORM

The old chimney was all that was left standing
   When all else was destroyed and gone
Once life surrounded this chimney
...The evidence of some family's home

The family that once lived there
   Enjoying the warmth of its fire
Sitting beside its hearth to enjoy
   Watching dancing flames aspire

The embers were stoked with the poker
   To incite a smoldering blaze
The smoke would curl up the chimney
   Floating as a cloud of gray haze
Continued

But a storm suddenly was brooding
...The menacing sky quickly darkened
The still winds vigorously, violently stirred
...To their sound beware and hearken

Scurry swiftly some shelter to find for
...Safety from the menacing storm somehow
The rickety old house couldn't protect them
...A safe place was needed now

The winds were billowing and roaring
...The sky resembling black tar
They could see the sky twisting and turning
...Forming spirals on the horizon afar

They dashed into the storm cellar
...Just barely in the nick of time
The storm came in fiercely and violently
...Like a vicious, great roaring lion

Everything in its path was taken
...Huffing and puffing until all was gone
Then quickly the storm left as fast as it came
...But all of their dreams were forlorn

When the storm passed quietness resumed
...They looked around but all they could see
Was one lone, proud chimney standing erect
...A replica of what their life used to be

The vista of that chimney on the horizon
...Offered hope to a family in disbelief
By standing erect and firm they could survive
...Their courage would conquer their grief
04.25.99

OH, GREAT AND MIGHTY OCEAN

Oh great and mighty ocean
Filled with such dynamic forceful motion
In early morning dawn you restlessly play
Then rest peacefully at the close of day

At times you frolic with the wind
Rolling and roaring with ceaseless end
Silvery ripples crease your brow
Unless your peace the wind should row

Then from the stillness of the sea
Cascading waters in playful glee
Lap against the rocks and shore
With gusty thrusts o'er them they soar

Your mood can easily changed again
If you're caressed by a gentle wind
Angry whitecaps will gradually cease
Relinquishing to a blissful peace

My love and I...and this playful sea
Are lured into mystic fantasy
We, too, are filled with intense emotion
Expressed by God's great mighty ocean
07.25.99

MY LOST POEM

I was filled with ecstasy
Walking quietly by the sea
Sand and shells inspiring me
To compose poetry by the sea

I had neither pen nor pad with me
So I set my poem to memory
Repeating the words constantly
Until the poem was part of me

Suddenly the quiet and tranquil sea
Tossed and turned angrily
It raged so fiercely it frightened me
Forcing the poem from my mind to flee

The waves swished in and covered me
And swept my poem right out to sea
No matter how hard I beg and plea
The poem will not return to me

The next time I walk down by the sea
I'll take a pen and pad with me
If the sea's fierce waves frighten me
I can rescue my poem for posterity
09.09.99

Dedicated to a day at the seashore...and my lost poem.

FOR THE LOVE OF THE LAKE

The lake provides a peaceful setting
Tranquil and serene as any place on earth
While listening to the gentle lapping of the waves
Dashing against the shore, flowing back again

Morning arrives slowly with a brisk breeze
There's plenty of time to nestle
Comfy on a deckchair with a cup of java
Or to lazily recline upon the sandy beach

Breathing in all the aromas and sounds
Absorbing all the beauty of God's incredible nature
Observing a simple display of wondrous marvels
That continuously change with the seasons

Pondering the dignity of the surrounding vistas
Visible across the rippling waters
It's intriguing to watch the antics of diving birds
As they swoop down upon their prey

Woolen blankets ward off the chill of morning
As the weather vacillates with incredulous whims
Never announcing its intentions or flexibility
As the day wavers toward its appointed end

Summertime offers long days and warmer nights
The indecisive climate's unpredictable approach
Disallows the lethargic spectator to envision fate's
Unforeseen summer shower spoiling an idle day

Nonetheless summer's essence is caught up
In the beauty of the lake and its rustic landscape
Neither rain nor sun spoils its intrepid inspiration
Nor the majestic lake's exquisiteness and splendor
04.23.99

THE MAGNIFICENT WATERFALL

The rushing of the waterfall
Flowing down the mountainside
Pouring forth energy's mystique
In which inspiring dreams abide

Spectacular dreams are quickening
Like swelling rivers flowing
Seeking novel expansions
Into new conquests it is going

Like our dreams building day after day
In the depth of the unknown
Until they overflow and drop into
Audacious places...there to roam

Dreams again launch forth stirring
New adventures, big and small
Like the conclusion of the descent
Of the uninhibited rushing waterfall

We all dream special mystic dreams
Making our lives exhilarating and thrilling
Next time you see a rushing waterfall
Remember that its adventure is enticing

Nothing's more thrilling and exciting
Than the magnificent rushing waterfall
To inspire and motivate us to be able
To conquer and to do anything at all
01.11.10

A LITTLE PATCH OF EARTH

What do you see in a little patch of earth?
Do you see its value? Do you know its worth?
Some don't have a vision of what it ought to be
A little patch of "dirt" is all that they can see

Others see unlimited and gigantic possibilities
Full of dreams and awesome mysteries
To them it's sweet ripe vegetables, row after row
Or maybe bright green pastures where cattle go

Visualize the scope of that patch of earth's ability
For things that make a mark on our future history
One man sees tall buildings reaching to the sky
Others a shopping mall with lots of things to buy

Visualize a sub-division, where happy families live
Churches and schools with people to help and give
Is a patch of earth to you just a bit of ground?
Or do you see a city, or maybe a little town?

Our forefathers had visions superior than most
Or we wouldn't have our nation for which boast
Next time you see a little patch of earth
Please visualize the splendor of its greatest worth
03.11.99

Psalm 24:1

"...The earth is the Lord's,
and all it contains,
The world, and those who
dwell in it.
For He founded it upon the seas,
And established it upon the rivers..."

MOON DANCE

The glow of the luminous moon
Completes a magical illusion
Of diamonds dancing on the waters
With a twinkling star infusion

Those romantically inclined
See the cascade across the sky
With its black velvet galaxy twinkling
A magical illusion to the eye

The moon's not really dancing
It's just sits there all aglow
It's our whimsical imagination
That can see this moon dance show

03.21.99

CLOUDS

Majestic castles in the sky
Formed by lazy clouds
Slowly floating by

Dramas continuing to change
Captivating my imagination
As lazy clouds begin to rearrange

Enchanting visions you can see
The clouds are secretly fulfilling
Your wildest fantasy

Running through the boundless skies
Frolicking against the blue
Presenting an ever new surprise

Sometimes the clouds passing by
Are gray and grumbly
Dropping raindrops from the sky
Continued

Clouds with a never ceasing wonder
With activities of phenomena
Accompanied by the roaring thunder

Then the clouds drift by aimlessly
Soon joined by the frisky winds
To romp and play frivolously

Lying there watching them
I am intensely mesmerized
By their every whim

They have such mystique
Covering up the sun
Then giving you a peek

Merry, merry little cloud
Overflowing with fun and laughter
Making all the heavens proud
07.29.98

THE FLICKERING FLAME

The flame flickered brightly over the log
   With exquisite beauty
   Inclined toward amorous affection

How comforting her warm glow
   Stirring every emotion
   Exciting the keenest senses

Her colors were rapidly changing and
   Swirls of smoke ascended
   Then disappeared into the brisk night air

Resembling a ballerina adapting an adagio tempo
   She lifts and spins and spirals
   Slowly climbing to the utmost heights

A breath of air sweeps down gently
   Causing her to impinge once more
   Passionately against his silhouette

She breaks into abrupt, staccato movements
   Without warning, like an adder's tongue
   She laps mercilessly at his soul

As though challenging him to an affaire d'houneur
   She wavers momentarily
   Dancing gracefully in the moonless night
Continued

Making hissing, crackling sounds
Shockingly disrespectful to the idle observer
She explodes into a mischievous, impish dance

Tantalizing his very heart and soul
She is conspicuously radiant
Awe-inspiring and alluring

Helpless against her effervescence
He succumbs to her embraces
And is left bleak and barren

Her scintillating flame dwindles into a faint flicker
Bestowing a farewell kiss with her flightiness
Ending abruptly

She quietly bids him adieu
Leaving a glow of her dying embers
A reflection of past splendor

He cries out for the relief of cool water
To squelch the ember's last breath
And release him forever from her grip
07.28.76

Notation: Sitting by the campfire in the brisk night air, observing
the flames caressing the slumbering logs as they succumb to her
passionate embrace and melt into ashes.

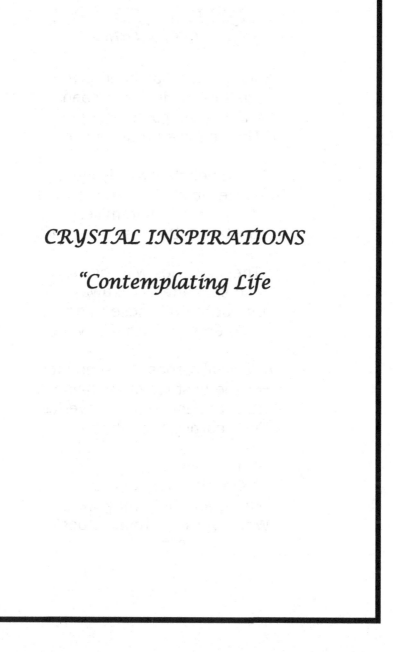

CRYSTAL INSPIRATIONS

"Contemplating Life

LIFE IS A GOOD WAY
To Spend Time

Each person has been given
The time of just one span
And told he could spend it
The best way that he can

Some people will misuse it
To booze-up and waste their life
Or spend it all in misery
In constant bitterness and strife

The lazy ones will choose
To squander it all away
By putting off those things
To do some other day

A few will choose to spend it
For the best for all mankind
With countless new discoveries
They earnestly seek to find

Some will stay real busy
Others relax and rest
Or do anything they want
Whatever they think is best

Continued

Some find unusual things to do
Or seek extraordinary places to go
All around the world they meet
Amazing people they want to know

Some will travel the world over
For all sorts of reasons...a facsimile
Of the changes in the weather
And diversity in the seasons

Adventure awaits us all
Or we can choose to be humdrum
There are opportunities for fame
And great riches for some

Life will have some sorrows
And sometimes there may be pain
But time is still worth spending
On life all the same

Consider this wise counsel
Keep this thought in mind
Life is really such a good way
For you to spend your time
09.16.87

LIFE IS LIKE
A Long-Playing Record

We live life like
A long-playing record
At any given point
We replay the same old chorus
Occasionally we change the words
But it's the same tune
Often the needle sticks
And repeats, repeats, repeats
We hear the same song
Until we are engulfed in its rut
What would happen if...by accident
We were to play the other side?
Would it really be
All the same?
Perhaps we need a new song
By a different singer...

09.29.72

TOMORROWS

Where are all of those tomorrows?
You promised me one or two
But it was only today again
When the sun came up anew

Where are all of those tomorrows?
I've been waiting for days and days
All those tomorrows turned out to be
Just a beaucoup of more todays

Today was Tomorrow, Yesterday

08.28.83

LIFE CONFUSES ME

I don't understand life at all
About the time I figure it out
Something else comes along
To change it all about

I'm familiar with Murphy's Law
As written in the books
"Nothing is as easy
As at first it looks"

Here's another observation
Which we surely must respect
"Everything takes longer
Than we first expect"

But one old adage is misleading
Which says, "You can't win them all"
And if you listen to it
It might bring you to a fall

What is more realistic
When your back's against the wall
Is for you to say, "It's true,
You cannot lose them all!"

Life is paradoxical
And your thinking, it can mar
'Cause you **can** lose a battle
Yet you still can win the war!

Now don't delude yourself
Into thinking otherwise
'Cause surely you must pay a price
Just to win the prize!

*Life confuses you
Well life confuses me, too!*
06.11.72

TAKE NOTE
And Remember This

This advice will never miss
If you take note and remember this
Each and every time you teach
There'll be someone you will reach

When you always do your best
To this certainty I can attest
Showing students your deep concern
Will inspire each one to learn

If you desire their best effects
Then always teach as God directs
To His truth you must attest
It's up to God to do the rest

I know this rule you have heard
It is your job to teach God's Word
The Holy Spirit then will give
The power to make God's Word live

THE FLIP SIDE OF TEACH IS LEARN
04.05.09

PSALM 119:11

"...Thy Word have I treasured
in my heart,
That I may not sin against Thee..."

NO MORE MONDAYS

I really wish we could get rid of
Mondays
I can't get ginning on such
Blue Days
Then the week could start on
Tuesdays
When Mondays are gone, we'll have so
Few days
Then Tuesdays would become our
Mondays
And soon we'd want to be rid of
Tuesdays
Then before we know it we would have
No days
Of course, we'd like to keep a
Few days
Like -- birthdays, holidays and
Pay days
But it might be nice to have no more
Work days

01.26.87

Dedicated to a serious discussion today regarding blue Mondays
with Michael Blaw, M.D., UTHSCD co-worker and friend, on
Monday, January 26, another...work day, blue day Monday. I am
just waiting for "pay-day, any holiday and my birthday!"

YESTERDAY, TODAY AND TOMORROW

All time comes together
As each person creates his own path
Winding where he wishes
Determining and cutting his personal trail

In solitude his mind wanders to his past
As an unpretentious child
Everywhere things have changed
Except in the eye of his mind

He remembers the past with deep impressions
Sometimes stronger than the original event
But he cannot stand still, nor wait for the world
To return to what it used to be

The debris of the past lingers
Once a vital link in the flow of events
But now its usefulness is lost reminding us
Yesterday has evolved into *today*
Continued

Life deals out one day at a time
Nevertheless we can use our days as we please
However we cannot retrieve the wasted days
But we can invest *today* into *tomorrow*

The future is not yet ours to have
But it excites our anticipation and our aspirations
The directions into *tomorrow* are diverse
But unreachable until we cut *today's* path first

Today was *tomorrow* -- *yesterday*
Even so, *today* will be *yesterday* -- *tomorrow*
The days all blend together gently
But then again all we really have is just -- *today*

So you must use *today* wisely
Always treat it as a friend
Thus you will not regret *yesterday*
Nor be afraid of *tomorrow*, my friend
11.24.74

OUR LIVES ARE A COLLECTION OF MOMENTS

Our lives are a collection of moments
  Some identify who we are
  Some define what we might become
  Some express what we have lost
  Some join us to others we love

Life is made up of one moment built upon another
  Moments we cherish
  Moments we dread
  Moments which seem like an eternity
  Moments which pass fleetingly by like a flash

Every day is a composition of changes
  Some days fly by without notice
  Some days linger far into the night
  Some days have various moments we let go
  Some days have diverse moments kept forever

What we do with the moments of our lives
  Depends upon our heritage
  Depends upon our environment
  Depends upon our experiences
  Depends upon our choices...mainly

Contemplating moments experienced, we realize
  Some moments creep slowly into our heart
  Some moments are embedded from the start
  Some moments grow with time and experiences
  Most moments depend wholly upon our *choice*
12.16.09

FOR EVERY DROP OF JOY

For every drop of joy
You leave along the way
Another drop of joy
Will return to you one day

For every drop of kindness
All the little things you do
One day in another way
They'll come back home to you

For every drop of God's benevolence
That one gives away to others
A closeness will develop
To make us all like brothers

For every drop of happiness
That you spread around
Happiness will seem to grow
Until its limit's found

Every drop of love you give away
Will fill another's cup -- and yours
It's just a part of Murphy's Law
That flowing love assures

For every drop of joy you give away
As you give them drop-by-drop
They will return to you again because
The flow of love and joy does not stop
03.12.06

ECCLESIASTES 11:1

*"...Cast your bread on the surface
of the waters, for you will find it
after many days..."*

INSPIRATIONS

What or who always touches you?
Is it an heirloom from the past?
Or is it a person who inspires you?
Who/what encourages you to do your best?

Maybe it's luxurious floral arrangements
That bring joy and stimulation into your life
Or perhaps an exquisite piece of sculpture
Carved by the artist's knife

A magnificent, shimmering tapestry
Hanging majestically on the wall
Anything that can catch your eye
Whether large or small

A spray of rosebuds; a fragile gown of silk
A gorgeous thing; a simple thing
Can endear itself to you
Until your heart begins to sing
Continued

Inspiration is all around us
In the sunset; in a child
At times it happens quickly
Sometimes it takes a while

Find what truly inspires you
To do your very best
Then let the mundane go
And keep your eye upon the rest

Don't fail to look around you
There's inspiration everywhere
When you discover and embrace it
Then you commence to truly care

The things that inspire us
Are the framework for our best
We can envision a project
But inspiration gives it zest
03.21.06

Dedication to Emery Tuttle and Crystal Elliot, the two people who
inspired me to do my very best.

DESTINY

Will I be swallowed up
in the infinite dark, black sea?
Or is there a better destiny for me?

Will I live and die short
Of a complete, abundant life?
Or will I settle for incessant strife?

What is my life all about?
What is the plan in store for me?
What in life can bring me harmony?

Will God desert me now
Before my time of life is through?
Or will He show me what His plan can do?

'Til now I've deliberately lived
In a stumbling, groping daze
Never wanting to seek Him or His ways

He promises to hear my despair
If I just cry out to Him in prayer
Because for me He does truly care
02.15.77

PSALM 48:13-14

*"...That you may tell it to the next
Generation For such is God
Our God is forever and ever;
He will guide us until death..."*

WHAT IS DESTINY?
My Questions

What is destiny?
Is it a place you have to go?
Ahead of time are you allowed to know?

What is destiny?
Is it predetermined for you and me?
Or can we say what it will be?

What is destiny?
Do events establish our life,
And decide between peace or strife?

What is destiny?
Is just fate our final destiny?
Or can we ascertain what our life will be?

What is destiny?
Does the seemingly inevitable have to be?
No! God gave free will to you and me
Our choice
03.18.06

FRIENDSHIP'S MOTIVATOR
(Count your Blessings)

Always remember to forget the things that
Made you sad
But never forget to remember the things that
Made you glad

Always remember to forget the friends
That proved untrue
But never forget to remember the friends
That stuck by you

Always remember to forget the troubles
Which have passed away
But never forget to remember the blessings
Which come each day

You must forget to remember the things
That made you sad
And remember to remember the things
That made you glad

Remember to remember and forget to forget
In the right way
Then you will be able to count all the blessings
You have received today
02.09.03

NUMBERS 6:24-26

"...The Lord bless you, and keep you,
The Lord make His face shine upon you,
And be gracious to you;
The Lord lift up His countenance upon you,
And give you peace..."

Have a Blessed Day

388

FROM THE PAST

French ribbons and roses
An art from the past
The era when women
Made treasures to last

Their lives seemed so simple
Homespun and handmade
They had heritage quilts, but
The patchwork would fade

Cooking and sewing by busy mothers
Sharing their love and real passions
The creations they made
Became the new fashions

Fine needlework with
Silk thread and wool yarn
When their clothing wore out
They'd make time to darn

I'd like to pass on
To my daughter or son
A beautiful treasure of
Patchwork I've done
03.21.06

Dedicated from one quilter to others.

I REMEMBER

When parades had confetti
And dimes were all silver
And coffee you got for
A nickel a cup

Park movies and snow cones
And Mickey Mouse watches
And trains that would run if
You just wound them up

There were ink wells on desktops
And children on playgrounds
And big, bright balloons that
You held in your hand

Tinkling charm bracelets
And streetcars and buses
And all the excitement
When TV began

Fourth of July fireworks
And Easter egg races
And all of our bicycles
Had only one speed
Continued

The old wringer washers
And sky-writing airplanes
And library books that you
Brought home to read

We had skating on sidewalks
And bought gum for a penny
And trips to the park when
Zoos there were all free

When swimming was public
And milk was delivered
And one car belonged
To each family

I like to remember
How things used to be
And recall all of those days
With fond memories
07.29.74

WHAT TIME IS IT?

What time is it?
We all have asked that question
Remember the old adage?
Today was Tomorrow, Yesterday

What time is it?
It's too late if the time was *yesterday*
It's too early if the time is *tomorrow*
We only have the time we have *today*

What time is it?
At birth we each are given a span of time
However we aren't told how long that span will be
The question is: How do we *want* to spend time?

What time is it?
Sometimes we waste our time
There are times we crowd it with too much activity
But always we spend our time by our choices
Continued

What time is it?
Do we say, "I don't have time today"
Or say, "I have too many things to do today"
Or do we make a different choice?

What time is it?
Time is according to where you are in that trilogy
Our only real time is the time to live our life *today*
So we always know what time it is...it's *now*
05.05.05

Dedicated to the day Emery asked me unexpectedly if I would like to go to the ocean for the day. The ocean has always been a place where I longed to go. But, my usual reply for such an unplanned, impromptu suggestion would ordinarily be, "I don't have *time; or, I have too much to do today." However, that particular day, instead of my usual reply, I made a different choice. I answered, "Yes, I'll be ready in one hour." As it turned out, it was one of the most wonderful experiences I have ever had. I am so glad that I made a different choice to use my time to go to the ocean that day. I hope I take a lesson from that experience and will always make choices that enrich my life. How we spend time is determined by our "choice," That lovely day, I spent my time at the ocean. Thank you, Emery, for giving me that opportunity to make a different choice.*

FAST TRACT

The world has gone off and left us
   Our lives are held in our *palm*
Pictures are taken by phone
   Power point controls all our plans

Food is put up in boxes
   Cars almost run by themselves
We instant message or e-mail
   Snail-mail is now obsolete

Oh we find ourselves on the fast tract
   We feel we've been left on the shelf
Oh if we want to keep up with the fast tract
   Then we have to get off of that shelf

Do we want to go back to the old life
   With horses and buggies and such
With everything handmade and homespun
   And bread made up from scratch

We walked to school in the snow
   And listened to gossip by phone
There were no fast-food stops on the corner
   And leftovers became our next meal

Oh we find ourselves on the fast tract
   We feel we've been left on the shelf
Oh, if we want to keep up with the fast tract
   Then we have to get off of that shelf
03.24.06

I'M RACING THE CLOCK

I'm racing the clock
And hurrying so fast
Tomorrow is my Birthday
Another year's past

Tomorrow I will be
A whole year older
Maybe by next year
I'll get a little bolder

I'll wear a few more feathers
And a lot more purple and red
Undoubtedly I will then begin
To turn everybody's head
07.31.08

Another birthday's already here. Oh how quickly the old year past.
But really, I'm not getting older...I'm just getting *BETTER* fast!

ECCLESIASTES 3:1

*"...There is an appointed time for
everything. And there is a time for
every event under heaven--A time
to give birth, and a time to die;...
a time to weep, and a time to laugh..."*

THE MONEY TREE

A long time ago a rumor was spread
This little thought was placed in my head
Money doesn't grow on trees, they said
You must work hard for every penny, instead

I didn't believe what I heard them expound
And wanted myself to check all around
So I looked in each store 'til one day I found
A money-tree seed to plant in the ground

It was certainly a strange and weird little seed
But I was proud the scoffers I didn't heed
I planted it, watered it and pulled every weed
Hoping a money-tree would grow from that seed

However it didn't pan out as I first thought
So I chunked all the seeds I had just bought
Now it was a terrible lesson I had been taught
But I had no one to blame; it was all my own fault

There's no money-tree seed -- that's a big joke
You buy *strange little seeds*, until you go broke
Disappointed you'll be 'til you just want to croak!
So I tell you don't fall for man's fictitious bloke

Now there is a secret how to make money grow
I'll tell you right now if you want really to know
It's a real paradox, so, I'll tell it real...s-l-o-w...
If you give God His money; your money will grow
.....*and that's the truth!*
06.03.83

396

VIEW FROM MY WINDOW

Out across the gloomy winter sky
   Somewhere the sun was setting
I wondered if I would ever know
   What would solve my intricate impasse

My sense of futility seemed so great, then
   I wondered why looking up into the sky
Even when it was gray and gloomy
   Could bring me a peacefulness and rest

Was it because I was looking at something
   Far greater than my finite self
Could I ever comprehend reality
   Would truth ever be within my grip

Was the solution in the problems or the questions
   Neither seemed to have a real answer for me
Was the answer in the inspiration of God's clouds
   Scurrying across the sky high above me

What does hold the answer for this dilemma
   What would bring me closer to a faithful God
I know God holds all life in His hands; and for me
   The answer I grasped was -- to trust God only
12.08.70

2 CHRONICLES 20:20

*"...put your trust in the
Lord your God; and you will
be established..."*

397

Tea leaves

Can we see the future
By tea leaves in a cup?
Or is life just by chance
And we'll never know what's up?

Impatiently we are waiting
To see each new day ahead
So curiosity compels us
To have the tea leaves read

For a glimpse into the future
To see what fate we hold
We're coerced by superstitions
To believe what'er we're told

What could be more harmless
Than a teacup full of leaves?
But can they tell the future
And all its mysteries?

The future might prove dreary
Or be purely asinine
Do we really want to know
What will come to pass in time?

We waited and we watched
As the last drop left the cup
What does the future hold?
What will the leaves turn up?

The tea leaves lay there quietly
Yet bold and quite defiant
Would they give their secrets up
To this inquisitive client?

Continued

Her bright and merciless eyes
Saw reluctantly what was there
Then hesitated a moment
And proceeded just to stare

An uncomfortable tension
Swept across the room
What did my future hold?
Was it full of gloom?

Suddenly her mood changed
A half-glint sparkle surged
Had my future changed?
A gleam of hope emerged

You cannot change the destiny
A soft-spoken voice announced
What will be...will always be
The future is pronounced

My plea became impatient
My curiosity was growing keen
Whether it be good or bad
Tell me – what have you just seen?

Nothing then -- but silence
I wondered what she'd do
Would she ever tell me
All the things she knew?

It was disconcerting
To stand there in suspense
Then she held her hand out
Please, give me...one sixpence
10.31.98

THE STREETWALKER'S LULLABY

What do you treasure?
What is your pleasure?
Is it a feather?
   Or could it be leather?

What do you want me to do?
Whatever it is, I'll do for you
From the time that we start
   Until we must part

You'll be happy, you see
When you come here to me
With one little wink
   I will tickle you pink

Or with this piece of fur
I will make you just "purrrr"
I can tie you to me
   So you can't get free

But I'm a very nice girl
So give me a whirl
What is your pleasure?
   What do you treasure?

Bring lots of money
When you come here, honey
'Cause girls like me
   Never come *free!*
11.30.89

Notation: This poem was not written from any true life or personal experience, except by the observation of the goings-on on Oaklawn Avenue in Dallas, Texas, and watching a little TV...lol.

WAR...

War is a terrible thing
Bringing heartache and pain
Everywhere men are dying
Lying there in the rain
War is a terrible, terrible thing

War is a terrible thing
Young men surrounded by fear
Bullets 'round them are flying
I wonder -- do they know God is near?
War is a terrible, terrible thing
03.21.06

Dedicated to all our men and women fighting anywhere in the
world to keep us free and to all those who have fought in days
gone by. May we honor the freedom they fought and died for that
we might be free.

CONSOLATION

Truly life is hard to bear
When tragedy's lurking here and there
But time has its mysterious ways
Of bringing us brighter days

Although now pain and grief you feel
Time soon will begin to heal
Your trust is in the Lord, just believe
Your pain in time He will relieve

To let you know for you I care
And in your sorrow I also share
Warm thoughts to you I today I send
Because you are my dearest friend
05.07.79

> "...Do not boast of knowing things that Nature attends to by herself, according to her order; but be delighted with knowing the end of those things that your mind conceives..."
> Leonardo de Vinci

A PHENOMENON

The sphincter of my mind
Binds my heart so tightly
That all life's blood ceases
all time stands still
all motions stored
I am then no more

Harnessing this powerful mind
Consciously taking control
Then an amazing phenomena starts
a deep awareness
a flash of creativity
That changes my destiny

The mirror of my mind
Reflects my dreaded fears
Or projects that perfect image
of all I ever wanted
of all I ever hoped to be
Extending life's breath eternally for me
08.27.79

HOPE SHARED

In the face of tragic news
  Hope continues to persist
Leaving the door ajar
  So endurance can exist

When caught up in a nightmare
  A small glimpse of hope sneaks in
Bringing a special promise
  Reviving life again

When things become most difficult
  That drop of hope is nourished
When the obstacle is impossible
  That faith in us will flourish

To share hope with those forlorn
  Is not to tell a *lie*
It's just to allow them enough *faith*
  To help them as they try

There is no greater anguish
  Than a person in despair
The best you can do for them
  Is let them know you care

Reinforce that hope in them
  Maintain it until they can choose
Within themselves to let sorrow go
  So their anguish they can loose
12.31.78

THE SAGA
OF THE H.D. TRAGEDY

Health, success and promise
That's what the future held
Then mysteriously things happened
And that bright future was dispelled

Vaguely at first it started
Then in a few short years
Life was all in tatters and
Filled with dreadful fears

A few attempts for help were made
But looking so disheveled
Some people thought him crazy
Others thought him evil

Life lost all of its meaning
Abandoned and forlorn
His quest for help unnoticed
He faced his loved ones' scorn

Years of terrible suffering
Plagued this lonely man
None recognized his problem
Or gave a helping hand

A very astute young doctor
Suspecting from what he could see
The problem was not drunkenness
But an illness was the key

This doctor tracked the records down
That confirmed his dread suspicion
Then helped this lonely man
Come to grips with his condition
Continued

404

The threat held by this disease
Had lurched unknown for years
Causing him much suffering
Loneliness, pain and fears

The puzzle was pieced together
But it was not the torment's end
For others could be affected
Who should from this man descend

Indeed it added weight
To his overwhelming sorrow
What about his children
And the children of tomorrow

There are some erroneous thoughts
As to what their future holds
Some or none could be affected
But which ones time alone unfolds

Sorrowfully it was explained to him
That once the illness had begun
It could not be reversed
Nor cured for anyone

But scientists the whole world over
Are searching constantly
Trying to find new answers
The cure that will set man free

Don't be discouraged the doctor added
As daily you learn to cope
Have patience for the future
Be not bereft of hope
05.07.79

Dedicated to R. Malcolm Stewart, M.D., UTHSCD, a young doctor
who has high hopes for the future cure of Huntington's Disease
(HD) and to his success in his research and his fight against
Huntington's and other neurological diseases.

MORE THAN A CONQUEROR

I walked a cobblestone path today
  With twists and turns along the way
Some of my steps were hard to make
  And some were even a great mistake

But along that path as I strolled
  Great adventures did unfold
When some turns brought me a difficult way
  Then a secret benefit would appear that day

I've always found the most tedious places
  Were profusely filled with God's sweetest graces
His hand was always near my own
  As His Grace flowed freely from His Throne

He'd pick me up and nudge me on
  Because He said I was His own
He bought me with a tremendous price
  His precious Son's own sacrifice

I still must walk along an unfamiliar path
  But now my heart can sing and laugh
Because I know what e'er befalls me
  My Heavenly Father will walk beside me

Victory's mine because I believe
  That His Son Jesus Christ died for me
More than a conqueror since God's Spirit's there
  More than a conqueror because My Lord cares
04.16.92

Dedicated to Frank and Nancy Schoenle, pastor friends who,
although their path became rough, they put all their faith in God
their Father to walk that path with them, and He did.

LIFE IS OUR STORY

Life is our story...
We write it page by page
Every event, every person in it has
An important part upon our stage

Life is a work of art...
Blank canvas awaiting an event
So our story can be painted
Showing how each day was spent

Life is an unwritten book...
Blank pages ready to record our tale
Moment by moment, day by day
Recording if we spent life well

Life is a melodious song...
With many verses to express our gladness
Some melodies are only tunes to be hummed
And we'll have a few verses to depict our sadness

Life is real drama...
Every player important for their role
Many characters will come and go
Their purpose only the final curtain will unfold

Life should be ongoing...
Where do you want your life to go?
Will you stagnate and let life stand still?
Or discover all that God wants you to know?

Life is your story...
Don't let others write it for you
Your path is made by **your** choices
So look to God to always guide you
09.06.10

NO REGRETS

Out of our longings for gratification
We are compelled to delude ourselves
Priding ourselves with our cleverness
We settle for an imaginary dream world

Unexpectedly the rut of life emerges
Able to prevail by the lack of challenge
Expanded by new experiences being abandoned
Extended by an adamant refusal to grow

Bitterness and dissatisfaction with life emanates
Enticed to jeopardize integrity
For one moment of pleasure
We were seduced by false hopes

Turbulence and pain swallow us up
Solemnly we contemplate what was at issue
But -- too late, too late -- contrition engulfs us
As we look back we repent -- regret

Faintly our heart is allayed
By a tiny ray of hope
Hope -- yes the sun *will rise* again
We *can* start afresh with no regrets
09.27.88

Notation: When we come to the end of our life, we need to be able to look back with no regrets.

SCRIPTURE REFERENCES:

All Scriptures are from the New American Standard Bible, The Open Bible Edition, Thomas Nelson, Publishers. New York

2 Chronicles 3:19; 20:20
1 Corinthians 11:26
Deuteronomy 6:5
Ecclesiastes 3:1
Ecclesiastes 11:1
Ephesians 4:32
Isaiah 6:3
Isaiah 26:3
Jeremiah 1:5
Jeremiah 29:11
Job 12:12
1 John 4:14-15
John 3:16
John 11:25-26
John 15:13
Luke 2:10-11
Mark 4:41
Mathew 6:21; 6:22; 6:25, 27
Matthew 16:2-3
Matthew 17:20
Matthew 18:3
Numbers 6:24-26
Philippians 4:6
Proverbs 17:17; 17:22;
Proverbs 31:10, 30
Psalm 24:1
Psalm 27:1
Psalm 46:10
Psalm 48:13-14
Psalm 51:17
Psalm 119:11
1 Timothy 2:3-6

MEET THE AUTHOR
JoAnne Tuttle

The author, JoAnne Tuttle, was born in 1934 in Fort Worth, Texas. She has three sons, Donald, Larry and David Holcomb. She attended Southwestern Baptist Theological Seminary in Fort Worth, graduating in 1965 with a bachelor degree in Christian Education. She worked for twenty years as an Administrative Services Officer for the University of Texas Health Science Center at Dallas, Southwestern Medical School (UTHSCD), retiring in 1994.

She married Emery Tuttle in 1971, attesting he is her soul-mate and her inspiration for adventure. Emery has three daughters and one son. Together, they have 18 grandchildren, 24 great-grandchildren and three great-great grand-children. However, JoAnne lays claim to being first to become a great-great grandmother; even so, Emery claims them as his, too

Continued

JoAnne has written poetry since childhood; but only in the past few years did she began to collect these poems from old envelopes, notebooks and scratch paper. etc., to compile them into a book. She also composes all of her own greeting cards.

Another hobby she loves is sewing. She especially loves making quilts for the grandbabies, family and friends. She enjoys doing scrap-crafting, making something from someone else's 'trash,' and calling it her "Renewed Treasures." She loves to travel, claiming "adventure" is her middle-name.

In 2001, at age 67, JoAnne attained her private pilot's license; three years after Emery acquired his license at age 76. Although, Emery was a WWII pilot, he had not flown in over 50 years and had to start fresh. Since obtaining their licenses, they have traveled the U.S. together in their Van single-engine-home-built RV-6A plane. Adventure is their cup of tea.

They designed and built their home at Cedar Creek Lake in 1991, and have enjoyed many projects and adventures together over the years. They are active in their church and community and their life's mission statement continues to be -- "It's not over 'til it's over."